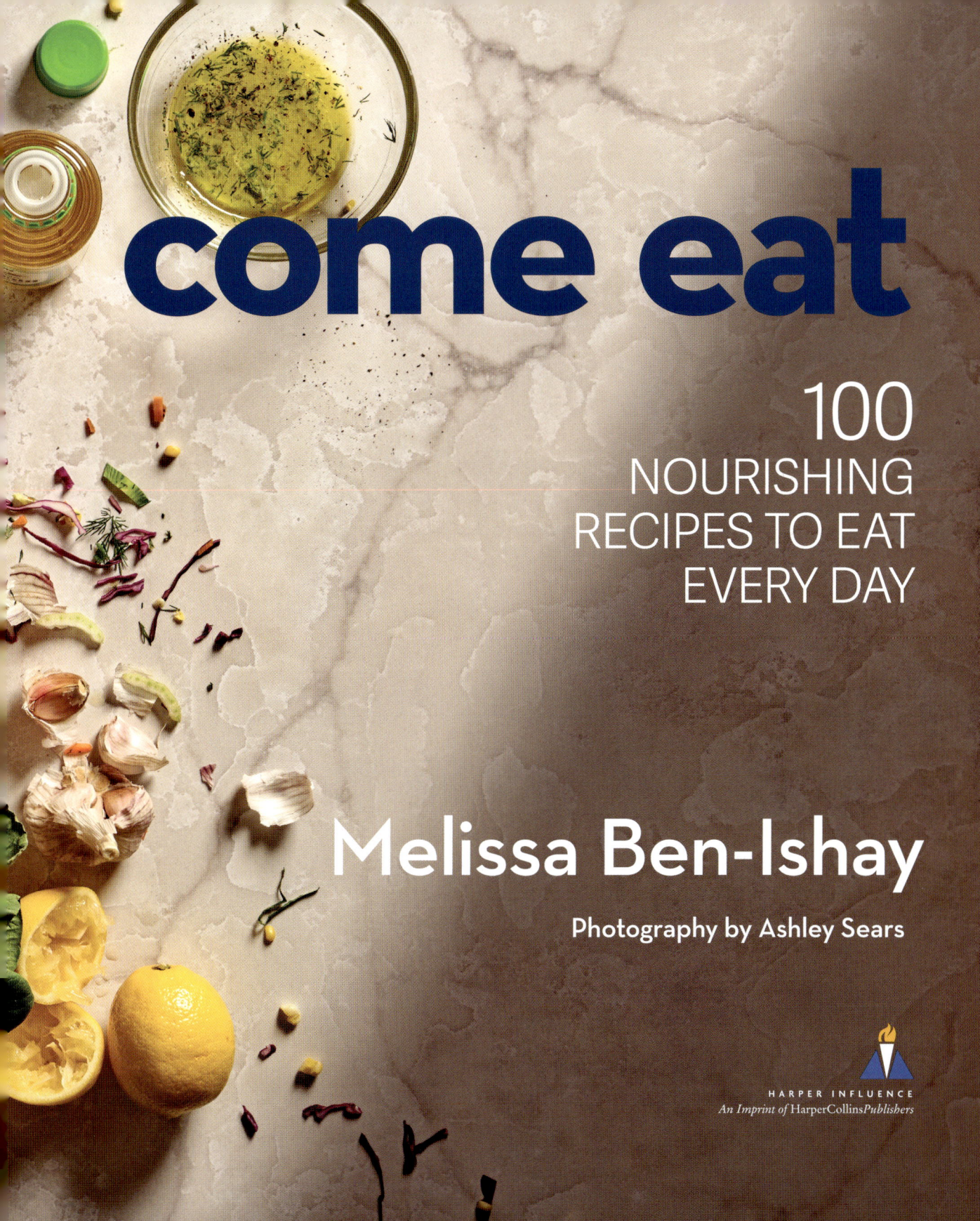

come eat

100 NOURISHING RECIPES TO EAT EVERY DAY

Melissa Ben-Ishay

Photography by Ashley Sears

HARPER INFLUENCE
An Imprint of HarperCollinsPublishers

To my parents
Thank you for every family dinner.
Now I get it—don't blink.

contents

introduction

When I was growing up, we had dinner as a family every night. It was a nonnegotiable for my parents. Obviously there were some exceptions, but most nights, my mom made dinner and the four of us—me, my brother, my dad, and my mom—gathered around the table to eat.

Every night, I helped prepare dinner (or dessert) and set and cleared the table with my mom. During the meal itself, I was encouraged to participate in conversation, but I also learned patience as my parents shared stories about our family and everyone discussed their day. Simply sitting around the table to eat dinner together taught me so many life skills that I'd take with me and continue to build on as the years passed: the art of conversation, showing interest in others, expressing love, and even how to deal with challenges—all while sharing a meal.

That kitchen table was sacred to my parents. At the time I didn't get it—how could I? But then one day, I went from being a kid to a mom myself. And I instantly understood all the values and lessons my parents worked so hard to instill in me, even when I didn't want to hear them.

The time we spent together around the table shaped me into the person and mother I am today. Along with everything else, our dinners sparked my love of food. Food—and the recipes in this book—are all about bringing the people you love most together around the table. It's about creating time and building connections. Sharing meals with my kids is sacred to me. It's my favorite part of the day. After a long day at work, I don't want to spend hours making dinner, so I've mastered the recipes that come together quickly and everyone in my family loves. I hope you and your family enjoy them just as much as we do.

As much as I love to shop at the market, I get my groceries delivered. On top of being a mom and content creator, I'm also the CEO of Baked by Melissa, the bite-size cupcake company I cofounded with my brother and a few others in 2008. It's a constant juggle. My groceries usually arrive early in the morning. My kids are at the age when they have activities nearly every day of the week, so my husband, Adi, and I often find ourselves alternating who makes dinner and who picks up the kids. My favorite days are when I'm in charge of dinner. After a long day of back-to-back meetings and putting out fires, I enjoy the process of cooking so much. Even when I'm rushing to get food on the table, there's something about preparing a meal that brings me peace, joy, and fulfillment. Dinner is one of the few moments we have together as a family. As soon as my kids walk through the door at the end of the day, they throw their bags down and I tell them to wash their hands and *come eat*.

Us at the Hoboken farmers market. We go every Saturday and get meat from Cotton Cattle Co.

We have a strict no-phones rule at the table (for me and Adi—my kids don't have phones yet) and love to play "rose, thorn, bud"—rose, the best part of your day; thorn, the worst; and bud, what you're most looking forward to. Sometimes we add a "learn," too. My kids often bicker about who gets to go first. And as anyone who has ever had a conversation with a six-year-old knows, sometimes this takes a long time. They hate being interrupted. But they're learning conversation, patience, and that they really do like broccoli, all at the same time.

Being a mom is the best. It's a combination of incredible love, challenges, and purpose. And it's completely magical. Women are superheroes, and society places unrealistic expectations on us. Between working full-time, doing the majority of the housework, and planning meals, it's just not humanly possible to do it all. I spend so much time thinking about what I'm going to feed my kids for every single meal. Of all the ways I provide for my family, this is probably one of the most difficult parts of being a mom.

> *I spend so much time thinking about what I'm going to feed my kids for every single meal . . . it's one of the most difficult parts of being a mom.*

Because of the nature of my job, I'm on social media a lot. I've posted a recipe video on the @bakedbymelissa account on Instagram and TikTok every day since April 2021 with no signs of stopping. As a creator, I love reading comments and seeing mouthwatering recipes from others. And, as I scroll, I'm constantly bombarded with information about which foods are good and which are bad, and what I'm doing wrong as a mom. It's information overload. The good part is that social media has also given me an incredible community of people who love food like I do and are looking for inspiration for nourishing meals. Thanks to this group, I've been able to spend more time in the kitchen, cooking dinner for my family as part of my job. It's market research, and some recipes test better than others.

Let's be real—I'm not making Spatchcock Chicken (page 169) for my family every day of the week. Adi cooks, too, and his Chicken Schnitzel (page 159) is on heavy rotation. Microwaved steamed broccoli is almost always on the table, and some days we make omelets or tortilla pizza. Or we order pizza or Chinese food. Then I have leftover rice and broccoli the next day to make Veggies & Eggs (page 196). Through the recipes in this book, I want to empower you to eat incredibly delicious meals and learn how to use the components again—sometimes in an even better way. Green Goddess Chicken Salad (page 78) is a great example of how a simple sauce can transform the leftover shredded chicken you have in the fridge.

I want the pages of this book to get dirty. Bookmark the meals that look appealing to you, then get really good at them. The more you cook, the easier it gets.

On occasion, I break our no-phones rule to look up health benefits to teach my kids. When my oldest was in first grade, I told her the specific health benefits of vegetables I served regularly—carrots and red bell peppers help your eyes, broccoli helps your heart, and protein (meat or vegetarian) keeps you full and makes you strong. That's when it clicked for her and she started expanding her palate. She's also started cooking for herself more, making herself eggs and smoothies and spinach and artichoke dip. Explaining the benefits of everything on her plate is the best thing we've ever done.

I regularly hear from so many of you that the way I cook vegetables has changed the way you and your family eats. I get messages on social media all the time from people saying

The more you cook, the easier it gets.

they never liked vegetables before, but after trying one of my recipes, their perspective shifted. One newsletter subscriber told me, "I've been trying to change my eating habits for years. You changed the way my family and I eat forever." Seeing the impact of my recipes continues to blow me away.

My schedule today looks different from my parents' day-to-day when they were raising my brother and me. But just like my mom, I make dinnertime a priority for my family. Our regular rotation includes recipes inspired by the meals she made for me growing up, from Sheet Pan Chicken (page 162) to Spaghetti & Meatballs with Magic Sauce (page 181) to My House Salad (page 40). Like most of us, I don't have as much time as as my mom did to prepare everything, so these recipes include tips and time-savers to make cooking for your family possible on even the busiest days. These dishes still take me right back to the kitchen table in the house I grew up in. And when I tell my young kids what's for dinner and hear them groan, I know that that's exactly how I responded to my mom (sorry, Mom). If your kids respond like this to you, you can't take it to heart. They'll get there.

Now, go wash your hands and come eat.

Melissa

salads

Salad, like dessert, has always been one of my favorite foods. As a kid, my mom served a big salad every night next to her spaghetti and meatballs or Oven Stuffer (as she says "Oven Stuffah"). It was often paired with Good Seasons Italian Dressing, which she made in one of those glass shakers with a plastic cap; sometimes it was a bottle of Seven Seas Creamy Italian, with little flecks of red and green in it (which were supposed to resemble vegetables?).

Back then, my love for salad had nothing to do with the fact that it's good for you. I think it was the crunchy vegetables paired with a delicious and indulgent dressing that I found so incredibly satisfying.

It's fun to think back on the meals I've loved most throughout the different chapters of my life. It's no surprise that salads have always been a main character. As a preteen, I'd walk into town with my friend Allison, and we'd spend our babysitting money on lunch at Friendly's. I'd get the crispy chicken salad served in a tortilla bowl you could eat. It wasn't the most nutritious salad, but man, it was delicious. Once we got old enough, our moms would drop us off at Paramus Park or Garden State Plaza mall, and the chicken salad at Joe's American Grill became my instant favorite. In college, my roommate Meri and I would pick up Greek salads with cut-up chicken fingers on top from the local restaurant Acropolis and eat them in our dorm. On weekends, I'd go sake bombing at Tokyo Seoul for their house salad (it inspired the Carrot & Ginger Dressing on page 39).

When I graduated college and moved to New York City, the grilled chicken salad at Hillstone (then, Houston's) became it for me. It still is, but I can't get there nearly as often as I used to. Shortly after moving to the city, I met Adi, and we bonded over our shared passion of feeding people we love. Sundays became our day to host friends and family for a meal, and thanks to this weekly ritual, my microchopped salads were born.

As I've grown up, started a business in the food space, honed my skills in the kitchen, and taken an interest in where our meals come from, I've learned a ton about food and the impact it has on our overall health. After all, food is the most primitive form of medicine.

Lucky for us, my salads check all the boxes. They're delicious, nutritious, fun to make, and great to share. The recipes I create include dressings that are just as good for you as the vegetables you pour them over. Realizing the best dressings consist of fat, acid, and flavor unlocked so many opportunities in my salad repertoire. I knew I could turn my love for this crunchy, refreshing staple into an entirely new level of spectacular dishes.

In this section, I'll teach you how to compose a salad with the correct ratios of veggies, crunch, and salty bite (page 11). Once you master the foundation, the world is your oyster.

How to Make Salad
(It's all about the ratios)

Once you understand the basics of how to build a salad, you can get creative with ingredients to make a salad designed to the specific tastes of you and your family or use what you have on hand. These are some of my favorites. Go crazy.

veggies

bell peppers, carrots, cucumbers, bok choy, edamame, broccoli, cauliflower, leftover roasted veggies, etc.

base

leafy greens, cabbage, kale, arugula, romaine, iceberg, etc.

Salty bite

cheese, olives, capers, etc.

Crunch

nuts, seeds, granola, tortilla chips, etc.

Confetti Greens

VEGAN, GLUTEN-FREE

15 minutes | Serves 4

Even though I'm known for my microchops, I didn't consider chopping arugula until pretty recently. It's so easy to throw in a salad bowl on its own, especially because it often comes pre-washed. Once I tried chopping it, there was no going back.

This is one of my favorite salads that I eat all the time. I really love the peppery flavor of arugula, and when you finely chop it, it becomes an entirely new green. An added bonus? You eat so much more of it when it's small. In this recipe, I dice cukes into equally tiny bits, toss in all the herbs I have in my fridge, and add olives for a salty bite. It's easy to make different variations of this salad based on what veggies I have on hand, but I always start with a base of arugula and cucumbers. And you know me—it's great on a chip, too!

6 mini cucumbers, trimmed
5 ounces arugula
1 cup pitted Castelvetrano olives
⅓ cup chopped fresh parsley
¼ cup chopped fresh cilantro

For a simple vinaigrette
¼ cup extra virgin olive oil
Juice of 1 lemon (about 3 tablespoons)
1 garlic clove, grated with a Microplane
1 teaspoon fine sea salt
¼ teaspoon black pepper
2 tablespoons white vinegar

1. Chop the cucumbers into confetti-size pieces (about ⅛-inch cubes), or as finely as you can. Finely chop the arugula and olives.

2. Add the cucumbers, chopped arugula, olives, and herbs to a bowl and mix to combine.

3. Make the vinaigrette: In a small bowl, whisk together the olive oil, lemon juice, garlic, salt, pepper, and vinegar. Pour the dressing over the salad and mix until everything is evenly coated.

4. Serve immediately and store any leftovers in the fridge in an airtight container for 1 to 2 days.

 Tip I love to serve leftovers on avocado toast with an egg on top.

Golden Girl Salad

VEGAN, GLUTEN-FREE

35 minutes | Serves 6 to 8

A few years ago, *Delish* asked me to create a new salad inspired by summer produce. I wanted the dressing to be different and catchy, so I brainstormed ways to make it creamy but vegan, like my Green Goddess dressing. Blending corn into the dressing was the perfect way to do it—the result was a bright-yellow, sweet, flavor-packed dressing that tastes so good you could drink it. This salad highlights all the colorful and in-season vegetables from the farmers market, covered in a creamy golden dressing. It's the perfect celebration of summer.

2 tablespoons fine sea salt

3 ears sweet corn, shucked

½ head green cabbage, finely shredded (1½ cups)

1 yellow bell pepper, seeds and ribs removed, finely chopped

1 bunch scallions, white and light green parts finely chopped

1 bunch chives, finely chopped

1 cup cherry tomatoes, halved lengthwise, cut into thirds

1 cup Sungold tomatoes, halved lengthwise, cut into thirds

Corn tortilla chips, to serve

For the creamy corn dressing

1 cup corn (reserved from above)

2 garlic cloves

¼ cup extra virgin olive oil

Juice of 2 lemons (about ⅓ cup)

2 tablespoons white vinegar

1 teaspoon fine sea salt

½ teaspoon black pepper

1 teaspoon garlic powder

½ teaspoon turmeric

1. Fill a large pot with cold water and add the salt. Set over high heat and add the corn. Bring to a rolling boil, then remove from the heat and cover the pot; set aside until ready to use.

2. Meanwhile, in a large bowl, combine the cabbage, bell pepper, scallions, chives, cherry tomatoes, and Sungold tomatoes.

3. Carefully remove the corn from the pot. Place the cob upright in a large bowl and anchor it with a fork, then cut the kernels off the cob. Reserve 1 cup of corn for the dressing and add the rest of the corn to the bowl with the vegetables.

4. To make the creamy corn dressing, in a high-powered blender (in this order), add the reserved 1 cup corn, garlic cloves, olive oil, lemon juice, vinegar, salt, pepper, garlic powder, and turmeric and blend until smooth.

5. Pour the dressing over the salad and toss to combine. Serve with chips, obviously.

Sweet & Salty Watermelon

VEGETARIAN, GLUTEN-FREE

15 minutes | Serves 4

If you know me, you know I do not put fruit in my salads. It's a rule I live by. Now, let me introduce you to the one salad that breaks that rule: my watermelon salad. It's the perfect salad for a hot summer day, when watermelon and corn are at their best. Between the salty feta, thirst-quenching watermelon, crunchy cucumbers, and sweet corn, it's nearly impossible for me not to eat the entire bowl as soon as I'm done making it. If you're like me and have an aversion to fruits in salads, make this. I promise you'll love it.

½ ripe watermelon

2 ears sweet corn, shucked

3 mini cucumbers

Juice of 1 lemon (about 3 tablespoons)

3 tablespoons extra virgin olive oil

½ teaspoon fine sea salt

½ cup crumbled feta

1. Cut the watermelon into ½-inch cubes and add to a large bowl.

2. Carefully cut the corn off the cob and add to the bowl with the watermelon. Cut the cucumber into ½-inch cubes and add to the bowl.

3. Squeeze the lemon directly over the salad and drizzle with the olive oil, then add the salt. Toss gently to coat the salad with the dressing, then top with the crumbled feta and gently mix. Serve immediately, while it's still cold. Store any leftovers in an airtight container in the fridge for up to 3 days.

 Tip I make this with the extra half of the watermelon that takes up space in our fridge when I buy them for our oldest. It's easy to double if you want to use a whole watermelon instead.

A Big Salad

VEGAN

45 minutes | Serves 6 to 8

This is my go-to salad for family holidays, and I love it for so many reasons. One, you can make it ahead of time (very important); two, it's super versatile and can appease a variety of appetites or dietary restrictions; and three, it only gets better as it sits. The ingredients I use each time are very dependent on what I have in my fridge, so if you're feeling adventurous, throw the rules out the window and make it how you want. Just choose your favorite grain, crunch, and salty bite—and have fun with it.

1 cup dry farro, rinsed
1 head green cabbage
1 small head bok choy
12 scallions, trimmed
4 mini cucumbers, trimmed
1 red bell pepper
3 medium carrots, peeled and trimmed
1 cup chopped fresh herbs (I used parsley, cilantro, and oregano)
1 cup shelled edamame
1 cup pumpkin seeds
1 cup sliced almonds

For the miso vinaigrette

Juice of 3 lemons (a little more than ½ cup)
¼ cup red wine vinegar
½ cup extra virgin olive oil
3 tablespoons white miso paste
1½ tablespoons dried oregano
1 teaspoon fine sea salt
1 teaspoon garlic powder
4 garlic cloves, grated with a Microplane
3 tablespoons nutritional yeast

How to Prep in Advance

1. Add the cooled farro, chopped cabbage, bok choy, scallions, cucumbers, bell pepper, edamame, and carrots to a bowl in individual piles. Wait to mix it together.

2. Prepare the crunchy topping and let cool, then transfer to an airtight container.

3. Whisk the dressing ingredients together and store in a jar with a lid.

4. You can do all of the above the day before. Right before you leave, chop the herbs and throw them on top of the vegetables.

5. When you arrive to the party, pour the dressing over the salad and mix well to evenly combine. Top with the toasted pumpkin seeds and almonds and serve.

continued

1. Bring 2 cups of water to a boil over high heat. Drain and rinse the farro, then add to the pot. Lower the heat to a simmer and cook for 30 to 35 minutes, until the farro is tender. Drain and set aside to cool.

2. Meanwhile, cut the vegetables. Finely chop the cabbage into small, confetti-size pieces and add to a large bowl.

3. Thinly slice the bok choy and scallions, finely chop the cucumbers and red bell pepper; add to the bowl. If you're making this ahead of time, try to give each vegetable their own corner of the bowl rather than mixing so they stay fresh longer.

4. Use a Y peeler to peel the carrots into ribbons, then roughly chop and add to the bowl. Finally, add the herbs, edamame, and cooled farro to the rest of the salad.

5. Heat a small frying pan over medium heat and add the pumpkin seeds and almonds. Cook for 3 to 5 minutes, tossing occasionally, so they don't burn, until they start to crackle and are slightly golden brown. Let cool, and store separately if making in advance.

6. Make the miso vinaigrette: Add the lemon juice, vinegar, olive oil, miso, oregano, sea salt, garlic powder, grated garlic, and nutritional yeast to a bowl or jar and whisk until combined. If making ahead, store separately.

7. Just before serving, pour the dressing over the salad and stir to get everything evenly coated. Top with toasted pumpkin seeds and almonds and get ready for the compliments to roll in.

Cukes & Beans

VEGAN, GLUTEN-FREE

20 minutes | Serves 2 to 4

When I'm craving string beans, I make this recipe inspired by Miznon, an Israeli restaurant founded by Eyal Shani that now has spots all over the world. At their Chelsea Market location, they toss their tender-yet-crunchy string beans in vinaigrette and serve them in a brown paper bag. I revel in their simplicity. Sometimes I splurge and order them when I'm at the office, but when I'm home, I love re-creating the recipe myself. Cucumbers seemed like a natural addition to transform this snack into a heartier salad. I could easily eat an entire bowl of this (and I absolutely have).

1 cup green beans, trimmed

5 mini cucumbers

For a simple vinaigrette

3 tablespoons extra virgin olive oil

1 teaspoon fine sea salt

¼ teaspoon black pepper

Juice of 1 lemon (about 3 tablespoons)

1 garlic clove, grated

3 tablespoons nutritional yeast

Splash of white vinegar

1. Bring a large pot of water to a boil and set up an ice bath.

2. Trim and cut the green beans into 1-inch pieces, then add the beans to the pot. Boil for 1 minute, then transfer to the ice bath to stop the cooking.

3. While the green beans cool, chop the cucumbers and add them to a large bowl.

4. Make the vinaigrette: In a small bowl, whisk together the olive oil, salt, pepper, lemon juice, garlic, nutritional yeast, and vinegar.

5. Add the green beans to the bowl with cucumbers and pour in the dressing. Mix to get the veggies evenly coated. Serve immediately.

Summer Salad

VEGAN, GLUTEN-FREE

45 minutes | Serves 4

I live for summer produce. There's nothing better than a big bowl of seasonal veggies from the farmers market. This is the kind of salad you want to slurp when you get to the bottom of the bowl, with all the juices and dressing mixing together. It's the best.

Our local market opens in May, and the early season feels like such a tease. I never leave with as much produce as I want to. In August and September, when the weather is warmer and we start to get bounty from local farms instead of greenhouses, I go crazy. I grab it all—tomatoes, corn, leafy greens, fresh herbs, anything and everything that looks good. Then I chop it all up (finely), throw it in a bowl, and add a simple, acidic vinaigrette to make the natural flavors pop. Just remember to serve this salad with a spoon so you can drink up all the delicious juices.

2 tablespoons fine sea salt

2 ears of sweet corn, shucked

2 pints cherry tomatoes

1 bunch scallions

5 to 6 bok choy leaves or 1 head baby bok choy

1 tablespoon fresh oregano, chopped

2 tablespoons fresh parsley

For a simple vinaigrette

¼ cup extra virgin olive oil

Juice of 2 lemons (about ⅓ cup)

1 garlic clove, grated with a Microplane

1 tablespoon rice vinegar

1 teaspoon fine sea salt

¼ teaspoon black pepper

1. Fill a large pot with cold water and add the salt. Set over high heat and add the corn. Bring to a rolling boil, then remove from heat and cover the pot; let sit for 5 to 10 minutes.

2. While the corn cooks, cut the tomatoes into thirds and add to a large bowl. Chop the light green and white parts of the scallions into ¼-inch pieces and slice the bok choy into thin ribbons. Chop the oregano and parsley. Add the scallions, bok choy, oregano, and parsley to the bowl.

3. Carefully remove the corn from the pot and cut the corn off the cob. Add the warm corn to the bowl with the veggies (the heat will help the aromatics bloom).

4. Make the vinaigrette: Add the olive oil, lemon juice, garlic, vinegar, salt, and pepper directly to the salad bowl and stir well to get everything coated. Serve immediately. Store any leftovers in an airtight container in the fridge for 1 to 2 days.

Miso Sesame Slaw with Crispy Tofu

VEGAN, GLUTEN-FREE

20 minutes | Serves 4

When I can't figure out what to make for lunch and find myself low on produce and time, I turn to this simple slaw. I often have a head of cabbage living in my fridge for weeks on end—it's amazing how long they stay fresh—and you don't need much else to make this drool-worthy salad. You can pair it with any protein you love, but if you think you don't like tofu, this recipe will change your mind. It's crispy, packed with flavor, and leaves you feeling satisfied.

For crispy tofu

1 block extra-firm tofu
3 tablespoons avocado oil
1 teaspoon sweet paprika
1 teaspoon onion powder
1 teaspoon garlic powder
1 teaspoon cumin
1 teaspoon fine sea salt
¼ teaspoon black pepper
½ teaspoon turmeric
2 garlic cloves, grated
¼ cup nutritional yeast
Avocado oil spray

For the slaw

1 green cabbage

For the miso sesame vinaigrette

Juice of 1 lemon (about 3 tablespoons)
2 tablespoons avocado oil
2 tablespoons toasted sesame oil
2 tablespoons white miso paste
½ teaspoon fine sea salt
¼ teaspoon black pepper
2 tablespoons white vinegar
2 garlic cloves, grated
2 tablespoons white sesame seeds

1. Preheat the oven to 425°F and line a baking sheet with parchment paper.

2. Start by making the tofu: Cut the tofu into ½-inch slices and press between two towels to get the excess moisture out.

3. In a large bowl, whisk together the avocado oil, paprika, onion powder, garlic powder, cumin, salt, pepper, turmeric, and garlic.

4. Add the tofu to the bowl and turn it to get evenly coated. Let sit for 10 to 15 minutes to absorb.

5. Sprinkle the nutritional yeast over the tofu and toss again to evenly coat.

6. Place the tofu on the prepared baking sheet and spray both sides with avocado oil.

7. Bake for 25 to 30 minutes, flipping halfway. The tofu should be golden and crispy on all sides.

continued

8. While the tofu cooks, make the slaw: Shred the cabbage with a mandoline, or finely chop. Place in a large bowl.

9. Make the miso sesame vinaigrette: In a small bowl, whisk together the lemon juice, avocado oil, toasted sesame oil, miso, salt, pepper, vinegar, and garlic.

10. Pour the dressing over the cabbage and mix well to combine.

11. Add the sesame seeds and stir.

12. Transfer the baked tofu to a plate and serve with the slaw. The slaw is a great condiment for sandwiches or tacos; store leftovers in an airtight container in the fridge for up to 3 days. For the tofu, store leftovers in an airtight container in the fridge and reheat in the oven at 425°F for 5 to 10 minutes until warmed through, so it stays crispy.

Crunchy Cashew Slaw

VEGETARIAN, GLUTEN-FREE

45 minutes | Serves 4 to 6

This salad is a project, and it's worth every ounce of effort. If you're like me and enjoy the process just as much—if not even more—than the output, this one's for you. It's in the same category as my Big Salad (page 18): great to make ahead, bring to gatherings, and works so well as leftovers. Each component—the slaw base, the dressing, and the brittle—is a recipe in and of itself. And together, they make for a wow-worthy salad that will become an instant favorite.

When I have extras from this salad, I like to use them as an ingredient in a bowl with sliced cukes, a big scoop of cottage cheese, and any other veggies I have in the fridge. The leftovers are even better than the first time you eat it and a gift to yourself the following day. Pro tip: Keep some of the cashew crunch topping to snack on all week long.

½ head green cabbage
½ head red cabbage
3 to 4 heads baby bok choy
1 red bell pepper
2 carrots, peeled and grated
3 mini cucumbers
½ cup parsley, chopped

¼ cup nutritional yeast
½ cup roasted, salted cashews
One 1-inch knob fresh ginger
2 teaspoons honey
1 teaspoon fine sea salt

For the cashew crunch

1 cup roasted, salted cashews
⅓ cup pumpkin seeds
¼ cup sesame seeds
1 tablespoon honey
½ teaspoon fine sea salt
2 tablespoons avocado oil
Black pepper

For the creamy cashew dressing

Juice of 2 lemons (about ⅓ cup)
2 garlic cloves
¼ cup extra virgin olive oil
2 tablespoons rice vinegar

How to Prep in Advance

1. Make the brittle 1 to 2 days in advance and leave out at room temp so it stays crispy.

2. Chop all your veggies the day before and store in an airtight container in the fridge.

3. Make the dressing and store separately in the fridge.

4. When you're ready to serve, thin out the dressing with water or lemon juice until it's a pourable consistency. Drizzle over the slaw and toss to combine.

5. Top with the brittle and serve immediately.

continued

1. Preheat the oven to 350°F and line a baking sheet with parchment paper.

2. Finely chop the green cabbage, red cabbage, bok choy, and red pepper and add to a large bowl.

3. Add the carrots, and cut the cucumbers into small, confetti-size pieces. (I do this by trimming off the ends, cutting them into ⅛-inch-thick slices, turning to slice into ⅛-inch-thick pieces the other way, and then chopping them into ⅛-inch cubes.)

4. Chop the parsley and add the cucumbers and parsley to the bowl. Stir to mix everything together.

5. Now, make the cashew crunch: Roughly chop the cashews and add them to a bowl with the pumpkin seeds, sesame seeds, honey, salt, and avocado oil. Season with a few turns of pepper.

6. Stir everything together with a spatula or spoon, to evenly coat with honey and oil.

7. Spread the mixture into a thin layer on the prepared pan.

8. Bake for 15 to 18 minutes, until golden brown. Let cool completely; it will harden into a brittle.

9. Break into small pieces and serve over salad, or just eat as a snack. If you don't use it all immediately, store at room temperature in an airtight container for up to a week.

10. While the topping is in the oven, make the dressing: Add the lemon juice, garlic, olive oil, vinegar, nutritional yeast, cashews, ginger, and honey to a blender and pulse to combine.

11. Scrape down the sides of the blender and add ¼ cup water. Blend again. Continue to add water, one tablespoon at a time, until the mixture is pourable but creamy.

12. Stir in the salt and adjust to taste.

13. To serve the slaw, pour the dressing over the salad in the mixing bowl and stir well to combine. Top with the crunchy cashew topping.

Taco Slaw

VEGETARIAN, GLUTEN-FREE

25 minutes | Serves 6 as a side

Sometimes when Adi and I set out to make dinner, we know what the protein is, but we don't know what else we're going to do. When this happens, for whatever reason, it almost always turns into tacos (well, our version of tacos). We'll cut chicken or steak into cubes and put them in a bowl, then slice up cucumbers and carrots or whatever fresh veggies we have on hand and throw it all on the table with a stack of flour tortillas. We almost always have a green cabbage in our fridge, and this slaw is so easy to put together with only a few pantry ingredients. This simple salad makes a protein-focused meal extra exciting. And it makes getting a dinner everyone loves on the table so much easier.

½ head green cabbage
½ head red cabbage (½ of each head or 1 whole cabbage)
¼ cup fresh cilantro

For a simple Dijon vinaigrette
¼ cup extra virgin olive oil
Juice of 2 lemons (about ⅓ cup)
2 tablespoons Dijon mustard
1 garlic clove, grated with a Microplane
¼ cup nutritional yeast
1 teaspoon fine sea salt
¼ teaspoon black pepper
2 teaspoons honey

1. Use a peeler to shred the cabbage. If you have extra bits you can't get to with a peeler, chop into small pieces with a knife.

2. Add the cabbage to a large bowl. Rinse and chop the cilantro and add it to the bowl.

3. Make the vinaigrette: In a small bowl, whisk together the olive oil, lemon juice, mustard, garlic, nutritional yeast, salt, and pepper.

4. Pour in the honey gradually as you combine all the other ingredients so it gets evenly mixed.

5. Coat the slaw in dressing and let sit for at least 5 minutes before serving. Store leftovers in an airtight container in the fridge for up to 3 days.

Cabbage Salad

VEGETARIAN, GLUTEN-FREE*

15 minutes | Serves 4 as a side

My go-to lunch when I'm working from home is a simple salad like this (it's also one of Adi's favorites). I make a huge batch and fill quart containers with it so we have salad all week long. It's the perfect blank canvas for leftover proteins. Hetty Lui McKinnon inspired the addition of Better than Bouillon (Hi, Hetty!), which keeps the dressing simple but adds delicious umami flavor. The dressing lends itself so well to ingredients I usually have in my fridge (cabbage, carrots, any protein) and my pantry (seeds, nuts). Have fun with it and use whatever you have on hand!

1 head green cabbage
3 carrots, peeled

For the sesame vinaigrette

1 teaspoon seasoned vegetable base
(like Better than Bouillon*)
2 tablespoons + 1 teaspoon toasted sesame oil
1 teaspoon fine sea salt
1 teaspoon white vinegar
Black pepper
Juice of ½ lemon (about 1½ tablespoons)
1 tablespoon sesame seeds

1. Use a peeler to shred the cabbage and add it to a large bowl.

2. Peel the carrots into thin ribbons, then roughly chop.

3. Make the sesame vinaigrette: In a small bowl, whisk together the vegetable base, sesame oil, salt, vinegar, a few turns of pepper, and the lemon juice, then pour over the slaw. Mix well to combine.

4. Add the sesame seeds and stir again. Serve on tacos, sandwiches, or wraps. Store leftovers in an airtight container in the fridge for up to 3 days.

Tip I love this salad with shredded leftover chicken, Crispy Tofu (page 27), or steak. Just throw your leftovers on top and you'll be a happy camper.

Note Make sure to check that the seasoned vegetable base you use is certified GF.

Brussels Slaw

VEGETARIAN, GLUTEN-FREE

1 hour | Serves 4

I grew up on salad dressing from a bottle. Creamy Italian, ranch, Russian dressing—you name it, I loved it. I can still taste them if I close my eyes. And while these dressings are delicious, they aren't nearly as nutritious as they should be. After all, you're making a salad. Why negate all the nutritional benefits by dousing it with a store-bought creamy dressing if you don't have to?

My passion for homemade dressings stems from my original love for these bottled dressings, but everything really shifted on my first trip to Israel with Adi, when his mom blew my mind with the simplest homemade salad dressing. It changed my life (and the way I make my salads) forever.

In this recipe, I use my simple vinaigrette as the base and add feta to make it creamy. It gets into all the nooks and crannies of the Brussels sprouts, which makes all the difference.

2 pounds Brussels sprouts
1½ cups sliced almonds

For the feta vinaigrette

1 cup feta
Juice of 2 lemons (about ⅓ cup)
¼ cup avocado oil
1 tablespoon white vinegar
1 teaspoon fine sea salt
1 garlic clove, grated with a Microplane
¼ teaspoon black pepper
1 teaspoon honey

1. Shave the Brussels into thin slivers with a mandoline.

2. Heat a frying pan over medium heat and add the almonds. Toast until fragrant and golden brown, 3 to 5 minutes. Pour the almonds on top of the Brussels sprouts.

3. Make the feta vinaigrette: In a small bowl, whisk together the feta, lemon juice, oil, vinegar, salt, garlic, pepper, and honey until the feta is mostly incorporated and pour over the salad. Mix well to combine. Serve immediately; store leftovers in an airtight container in the refrigerator for 1 to 2 days.

Carrot & Ginger Dressing on Iceberg

VEGAN, GLUTEN-FREE

15 minutes | Serves 4 to 6

This was one of the first salads I fell in love with—the often-free house salad you get at a Japanese restaurant. As a kid, whenever my family ordered sushi, it was what I was most excited about. In college, I'd go sake bombing with my friends at Tokyo Seoul in Syracuse to have an excuse to eat iceberg covered in my favorite orange dressing, removing the single cherry tomato on top before diving in.

Recently, I was craving the nostalgic dressing and decided to try to make it myself. It was so easy. To add extra nutrients, I supercharged the dressing with extra citrus, fresh ginger, and turmeric. This dressing will always be one of my all-time faves—especially now that I can make it at home in just a few minutes.

1 head iceberg lettuce

For the carrot & ginger dressing

3 carrots, peeled and cut into 1-inch pieces
Juice of 2 lemons (about ⅓ cup)
1 tablespoon + 1 teaspoon white miso paste
2 tablespoons toasted sesame oil
¼ cup rice vinegar
¼ cup extra virgin olive oil
One 1-inch knob ginger, peeled
One 2-inch knob fresh turmeric, peeled
¼ yellow onion
1 teaspoon fine sea salt
Black pepper

1. Wash the iceberg and cut into 1-inch squares.

2. Make the dressing: Add the carrots, lemon juice, miso, sesame oil, vinegar, olive oil, ginger, turmeric, onion, salt, and a few turns of pepper to a blender and pulse until smooth. It will still be thick.

3. Pour the dressing over the iceberg and serve. Store dressing leftovers in an airtight container in the fridge for 3 to 5 days.

My House Salad

VEGETARIAN*

30 minutes | Serves 4

This is an essential salad to have in your rotation. It's inspired by salad you'd get at a steakhouse. It always reminds me of the bibb salad at Union Square Café in New York City, because it's simple and delicious, with a dressing that makes you want to eat a huge bowl of lettuce. It's a very easy salad to make, but it also looks really impressive. I love the method of cutting a tortilla into pieces and toasting them in a pan with garlic, oil, and salt for the perfect crunch to top your salad, and added a seven-minute egg to make it a meal.

2 large eggs
2 tablespoons extra virgin olive oil
Two 8-inch flour tortillas
½ teaspoon fine sea salt
½ teaspoon garlic powder
1 radish, thinly sliced
2 mini cucumbers
1 shallot
5 ounces baby butter lettuce

For the herby vinaigrette

Juice of 1 lemon (about 3 tablespoons)
3 tablespoons extra virgin olive oil
½ teaspoon fine sea salt
¼ teaspoon black pepper
1 tablespoon white vinegar
2 garlic cloves, grated
1 teaspoon fresh, chopped dill

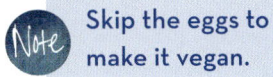 **Note** Skip the eggs to make it vegan.

1. Boil a large pot of water over high heat. Once it comes to a rolling boil, add the eggs. Prepare an ice bath.

2. Cook the eggs for 7 minutes, then immediately transfer to the ice bath to stop the cooking. After at least a minute, peel the eggs and cut in half lengthwise.

3. While the eggs cook, add the olive oil to a small frying pan over medium-high heat. Cut the tortilla into small rectangles, about ½ inch × 1 inch. Add the tortilla pieces to the pan and stir to evenly coat in the oil. Season with the salt and cook until the tortillas are golden brown, 2 to 3 minutes, tossing occasionally so they don't burn. When the tortillas are almost finished, add the garlic powder and transfer to a mixing bowl.

4. Thinly slice the radish then cut it into matchsticks. Finely chop the cucumbers and thinly slice the shallot. Add the radish, cucumbers, shallot, and lettuce to a large bowl.

5. Make the herby vinaigrette: In a small bowl, whisk together the lemon juice, olive oil, salt, pepper, vinegar, garlic, and dill. Pour the dressing over the salad and toss to evenly coat.

6. Serve with the halved soft-boiled eggs and crunchy tortillas on top. This is best enjoyed immediately.

Seder Caesar

VEGAN

45 minutes | Serves 6 as a side

If you're Jewish and celebrate Passover, there's a week every year you can't eat bread. Enter matzo. Matzo is used for all sorts of dishes during Passover, like matzo brei with eggs or matzo crack with toffee and chocolate. I don't like matzo because it gives me a stomachache. You can absolutely make a salad without croutons—or use a different ingredient to add crunch like nuts or seeds— but this garlicky matzo is a conversation starter and it's fun for Passover. The salad itself is simple to make and will leave you feeling great. Which after a week of matzo, you'll be craving. L'Chaim!

For the salad

1 bunch dino kale

1 bunch baby bok choy

1 pound Brussels sprouts

1 bunch scallions, trimmed and sliced into ¼-inch pieces

For the matzo topping

3 pieces matzo

3 tablespoons extra virgin olive oil

3 garlic cloves, grated with a Microplane

2 teaspoons za'atar

Fine sea salt

For the vegan Caesar dressing

2 garlic cloves

Juice of 2 lemons (about ⅓ cup)

¼ cup extra virgin olive oil

1 teaspoon fine sea salt

¼ teaspoon black pepper

¼ cup tahini

2 tablespoons white vinegar

1 tablespoon capers with juice

1 cup canned chickpeas, drained and rinsed

¼ cup nutritional yeast

1 teaspoon garlic powder

1 tablespoon Dijon mustard

1. Make the salad: Remove the fibrous stems from the kale. Thinly slice the kale and bok choy into thin ribbons about ⅛ inch thick. With a mandoline, thinly slice the Brussels sprouts. Combine the greens and scallions in a large bowl.

2. Make the matzo topping: Break the matzo into small pieces with your hands. Heat the oil with the garlic in a pan over medium heat, stirring occasionally.

3. After about 2 minutes, add the matzo, tossing occasionally so it doesn't burn. Cook until the matzo is nice and toasted, 5 to 10 minutes. Add the za'atar and season with salt to taste. Transfer to a bowl to stop the cooking.

4. Make the Caesar dressing: Add the garlic, lemon juice, oil, salt, pepper, tahini, vinegar, capers and their juices, chickpeas, yeast, garlic powder, and mustard to a blender and pulse until smooth.

5. Pour the dressing over the greens, 1 cup at a time, mixing well to evenly coat.

6. Top with the garlicky matzo just before serving. Store any leftovers in an airtight container in the fridge for 2 to 3 days.

Kale with Garlicky Croutons

VEGETARIAN

45 minutes | Serves 4

I know there's a lot of talk about massaging your kale, but if you cut it small enough, there's no need. When I'm cooking with kale, I roll it up and slice it into thin strips, until it looks almost like grass. Then I'll cut it in the opposite direction to make the pieces shorter. The smaller the kale, the more you eat! And it makes it so much easier to chew and digest.

This is a great salad for winter gatherings, since you can easily make it ahead of time. Swap out the snap peas for edamame and the corn for bell peppers if they're easier to come by. I find turning day-old sourdough into something entirely new and different so satisfying, and the croutons in this recipe are a favorite. Once you make them yourself, you'll never buy croutons from the store again.

1 bunch dino kale

2 candy cane beets

2 carrots, peeled

5 to 6 sugar snap peas

2 cobs sweet corn, shucked

For the croutons

¼ cup extra virgin olive oil

2 garlic cloves, grated

4 slices day-old sourdough bread

½ teaspoon fine sea salt

For the honey mustard vinaigrette

1 tablespoon white vinegar

1 teaspoon honey

1 tablespoon Dijon mustard

¼ teaspoon black pepper

Juice of 1 lemon (about 3 tablespoons)

1 teaspoon fine sea salt

1 garlic clove, grated

¼ cup extra virgin olive oil

1. Remove the fibrous stems from the kale and roll each leaf away from you. Chop first into long strips, then turn and chop widthwise.

2. Peel the beets and cut them into matchsticks. Use the wide holes of a box grater to grate the carrots, and mandoline or thinly slice the snap peas. Cut the corn off the cob.

3. Add all of the veggies to a large bowl.

4. Make the croutons: Heat the olive oil in a large skillet and add the garlic. Cut the bread into ¾-inch cubes and add it to the pan.

5. Toast the bread on all sides until golden brown, about 3 to 5 minutes on either side, then season with the salt.

6. Make the honey mustard vinaigrette: In a small bowl, whisk together the vinegar, honey, mustard, pepper, lemon juice, salt, garlic, and oil until emulsified, then pour over the salad. Mix well to fully coat everything in the dressing.

7. Serve the salad with the croutons. Store any leftovers in an airtight container in the fridge for up to 2 days.

Panzanella

VEGAN

25 minutes | Serves 4

I won't order a panzanella when I see it on a menu. I'm so picky about tomatoes—I need to know they're ripe and flavorful, which only really happens when I choose them myself. The one place I break this rule is in Israel, when we visit Adi's family. The tomatoes there are always in-season and burst with the most amazing flavor. I ordered a panzanella for the first time at a restaurant in a strip mall not far from Adi's parents' house and it was incredible. As soon as I took my first bite, I knew I needed to make it when I got home. The crunchy fried bread soaks up all the juices, creating the most delicious, simple salad. Tomatoes are the most important ingredient, so be very choosy with them. If you think you don't like tomatoes, you probably just haven't had a good one yet.

2 cups bread (about ⅓ standard sourdough loaf)

¼ cup extra virgin olive oil

1 teaspoon garlic powder

½ teaspoon fine sea salt

¼ teaspoon black pepper

2 pints cherry tomatoes

½ red onion, thinly sliced

1 teaspoon fresh oregano

For the vinaigrette

¼ cup extra virgin olive oil

Juice of 1 lemon (about 3 tablespoons)

3 tablespoons red wine vinegar

1 teaspoon fine sea salt

1 teaspoon dried oregano

2 tablespoons nutritional yeast

1 garlic clove, grated with a Microplane

¼ teaspoon black pepper

1. Preheat an air fryer to 400°F or a standard oven to 425°F. Rip the sourdough into roughly 1-inch pieces and place them in a large bowl. Cover with the olive oil, garlic powder, salt, and pepper. Use your hands to combine.

2. Cook the bread 10 minutes in an air fryer or 12 to 15 minutes in a standard oven until golden brown, keeping a close eye on it. Check often, tossing occasionally so the bread toasts evenly. Let cool.

3. Slice the tomatoes into thirds and add them to the same bowl that you mixed the bread in. Use a mandoline to thinly slice the onion; stir the onion into the bowl with tomatoes. Add the fresh oregano and stir to combine.

4. Make the vinaigrette: In a small bowl, whisk together the oil, lemon juice, vinegar, salt, dried oregano, nutritional yeast, garlic, and pepper.

5. Pour the dressing over the tomatoes and toss to combine.

6. Add the bread pieces to the tomato mixture so they get covered with the tomato juices and the dressing. Serve immediately.

Greek Goddess

GLUTEN-FREE

25 minutes | Serves 4

I love Greek salads, but there are certain elements to them that I don't love. I'm very particular about tomatoes, even when they're in season, so I usually leave them out. I find red onion to be very sharp, so I usually skip that, too. This is my perfect Greek salad—it's so simple and filled with Mediterranean flavors, even if the ingredients aren't typically what you'd think of when you imagine the classic recipe. We always have a can of dolmas (stuffed grape leaves) in the pantry; you should try them if you've been holding out. They're so delicious! I love adding them to this salad. They're filling and add the perfect salty bite.

2 heads romaine lettuce

4 mini cucumbers

8 to 10 pitted Kalamata olives

¼ cup feta

1 teaspoon za'atar

7-ounce can dolmas (stuffed grape leaves)

For the miso vinaigrette

⅓ cup extra virgin olive oil

Juice of 2 lemons (about ⅓ cup)

¼ cup red wine vinegar

¼ cup white miso paste

⅓ cup nutritional yeast

1 tablespoon dried oregano

2 garlic cloves, grated with a Microplane

½ teaspoon fine sea salt

Black pepper

1. Finely chop the romaine, cucumbers, and olives and place in a large bowl.

2. Make the miso vinaigrette: In a small bowl, whisk together the olive oil, lemon juice, vinegar, miso, nutritional yeast, oregano, garlic, salt, and a few turns of pepper until emulsified. Pour over the salad and mix well to combine.

3. Top with the feta, za'atar, and dolmas. Serve immediately.

Greek Lentil Salad

VEGAN, GLUTEN-FREE

30 minutes | Serves 4

I don't cook with lentils nearly as often as I should. Lentils are so nutritious—they're high in fiber, protein, iron, B vitamins, antioxidants, and so much more. I first made this salad because I had random vegetables in my fridge but also wanted to make a hearty salad. Cue the lentils. Everything works so well together in this dish. It's great as a full, colorful meal when you have friends coming over since it's so easy to make ahead of time.

1 cup dry brown lentils

3 cups vegetable broth

3 mini sweet peppers: red, orange, and yellow

5 ounces arugula

3 mini cucumbers

3 to 4 scallions, trimmed

1 cup pitted Kalamata olives

For the miso vinaigrette

⅓ cup extra virgin olive oil

Juice of 2 lemons (about ⅓ cup)

¼ cup red wine vinegar

¼ cup white miso paste

⅓ cup nutritional yeast

1 tablespoon dried oregano

2 garlic cloves, grated with a Microplane

½ teaspoon fine sea salt

Black pepper

1. Rinse the lentils in a fine-mesh strainer and pick over for loose stones and debris. Add the broth to a small saucepan over medium-high heat. Add the lentils and bring to a simmer. Cover the pot and cook until the lentils are tender, 15 to 20 minutes.

2. If there's still a lot of broth that hasn't been absorbed into the lentils, drain the lentils using a fine-mesh strainer. Transfer to a bowl to cool.

3. While the lentils cook, finely chop the peppers, arugula, cucumbers, scallions, and olives, and add them to a large bowl.

4. Make the miso vinaigrette: In a small bowl, whisk together the olive oil, lemon juice, vinegar, miso, nutritional yeast, oregano, garlic, salt, and a few turns of pepper until smooth.

5. Add the cooked lentils to the bowl and stir to combine.

6. Pour the dressing over the salad and mix well so everything is covered.

7. Serve as a side or as a full meal; if serving as a meal, I like to add a fried egg on top for extra protein. Store leftovers in an airtight container in the fridge for 3 to 5 days.

Mediterranean Couscous Salad

VEGAN

30 minutes | Serves 4

Thanks to my husband, I gravitate toward ingredients that transport us to my mother-in-law's kitchen near the Mediterranean. Covering the aromatics with warm zucchini helps bloom the garlic and herbs; the tomato juice mixes with the dressing; couscous absorbs all the delicious flavors. Pure summer magic. This is a great way to use any leftover couscous (or grain) you have. Top it with whatever protein you love and you've got yourself a whole meal.

½ cup dry couscous (Moroccan-style, not Israeli or pearl)

½ teaspoon extra virgin olive oil

¼ teaspoon salt

1 tablespoon avocado oil

2 zucchini, trimmed and diced

1 garlic clove, grated with a Microplane

¾ teaspoon fine sea salt

1 teaspoon dried oregano

1 red bell pepper, diced

½ cup pitted Kalamata olives

One 6.5 ounce jar artichoke hearts, drained

1 cup small tomatoes, like cherry, grape, or on the vine (use whatever looks best)

1 bunch scallions, trimmed

⅓ cup parsley, chopped

For a simple vinaigrette

¼ cup extra virgin olive oil

Juice of 2 lemons (about ⅓ cup)

1 teaspoon fine sea salt

¼ teaspoon black pepper

2 teaspoons dried oregano

2 tablespoons red wine vinegar

1 teaspoon garlic powder

2 garlic cloves, grated with a Microplane

1. Set ½ cup water over high heat in a small pot. Stir in the couscous, olive oil, and salt and cover the pot. Once boiling, remove the pot from heat and let stand for 5 minutes.

2. Uncover the pot and fluff the couscous with a fork. Let cool.

3. Heat the avocado oil in a large frying pan over medium-high heat. Add the zucchini to the pan with the garlic, salt, pepper, and oregano; stir. Sauté until tender but not translucent, 3 to 5 minutes. Transfer the zucchini to a large bowl and stir in the couscous.

4. Roughly chop the red pepper, olives, and artichoke hearts and add to the bowl.

5. Cut the tomatoes into quarters and chop the scallions. Add the tomatoes, scallions, and parsley to the bowl.

6. Make the vinaigrette: In a small bowl, whisk together the olive oil, lemon juice, salt, pepper, oregano, vinegar, garlic powder, and garlic cloves.

7. Pour the dressing over the salad and mix well to combine. Serve immediately; store any leftovers in an airtight container in the fridge for 3 to 5 days.

Farro & Veggies

VEGETARIAN

45 minutes | Serves 4 to 6

This salad lives in the "make ahead and bring with you to parties" category. (Or, similarly, the "easy hosting recipes" category.) I love salads that have grains in them, and farro has a nice chew. It's naturally al dente and packed with fiber and protein to keep you full. The grain is the perfect size to pair with microchopped veggies, because it supports getting the perfect ratio of flavors in every bite—a little grain, a little veg, and a little creamy feta. It hits all the notes.

1 cup dry farro, rinsed
1 teaspoon fine sea salt
1 cup snap peas, trimmed
4 scallions, trimmed
1 red bell pepper
3 mini cucumbers
1 pint cherry tomatoes
½ small red cabbage, shredded (about 1 cup)
4 ounces feta

For the miso vinaigrette

⅓ cup extra virgin olive oil
Juice of 2 lemons (about ⅓ cup)
¼ cup red wine vinegar
¼ cup white miso paste
⅓ cup nutritional yeast
1 tablespoon dried oregano
2 garlic cloves, grated with a Microplane
½ teaspoon fine sea salt
Black pepper

1. Bring 3 cups of water to a boil over high heat. Add the salt to the water and add the rinsed farro. Return the water to a boil, then reduce heat for a steady simmer. Cook for 25 to 30 minutes, until the farro is chewy and tender. Drain using a fine-mesh strainer and set aside to cool.

2. While the farro cooks, cut the snap peas and scallions into ¼-inch pieces on a bias and finely chop the bell pepper and cucumbers.

3. Cut the tomatoes in half lengthwise, then into thirds.

4. Add the cooked farro, snap peas, scallions, bell pepper, cucumbers, tomatoes, and cabbage to a large bowl.

5. Make the miso vinaigrette: In a small bowl, whisk together the oil, lemon juice, vinegar, miso, nutritional yeast, oregano, garlic, salt, and a few turns of pepper until completely emulsified.

6. Pour the dressing over the salad (you may have extra—only add as much as you think the salad needs based on your taste preferences, and save the rest in the fridge for something else). Stir to combine.

7. Crumble the feta with your hands and add on top of the salad just before serving. Store leftovers in an airtight container in the fridge for up to 3 days.

Brussels & Potatoes

VEGETARIAN, GLUTEN-FREE

1 hour 15 minutes | Serves 4

Anyone who has ever used a mandoline has a war story. Please be careful. We don't need any more finger nicks.

 I used potatoes for croutons because I had them, but it's a great hack when you want something new or gluten-free. Just between us, miso vinaigrette is the best dressing I make. Whip up a big jar of it and keep it in your fridge—you'll want to drink it.

4 Yukon Gold potatoes
 (about 2 pounds)

2 tablespoons extra virgin
 olive oil, plus more
 as needed

3 garlic cloves, grated

½ teaspoon fine sea salt

¼ teaspoon black pepper

½ teaspoon dried oregano

½ cup freshly grated Parmesan

2 pounds Brussels sprouts

For the miso vinaigrette

⅓ cup extra virgin olive oil

Juice of 2 lemons
 (about ⅓ cup)

¼ cup red wine vinegar

¼ cup white miso paste

⅓ cup nutritional yeast

1 tablespoon dried oregano

2 garlic cloves, grated with
 a Microplane

½ teaspoon fine sea salt

Black pepper

1. Preheat the oven to 450°F and line a baking sheet with parchment paper.

2. Cut the potatoes into ½-inch cubes (you should have about 3 cups). Place them in a large bowl.

3. Add the olive oil, garlic, salt, pepper, oregano, and Parmesan to the bowl. Mix well.

4. Once you've given it a good stir, make sure the Parmesan is covered in oil. If not, add a bit more oil, 1 teaspoon at a time. The potatoes should be evenly coated with a shiny coating of olive oil, cheese, and spices.

5. Spread the potatoes evenly on the parchment and bake for 1 hour, flipping halfway through. Remove from the oven when they're deep golden, and let cool.

6. While the potatoes cook, prepare the rest of the salad. Using a mandoline, shred the Brussels sprouts into thin ribbons. Add to a large bowl.

7. Make the miso vinaigrette: In a small bowl, whisk together the olive oil, lemon juice, vinegar, miso, nutritional yeast, oregano, garlic, salt, and a few turns of pepper until emulsified.

8. Just before serving, pour the dressing over the Brussels sprouts and mix well to combine. Top with the crispy potatoes to serve. Store leftovers in an airtight container in the fridge for 2 to 3 days.

Sheet Pan Salad

VEGAN, GLUTEN-FREE

1 hour | Serves 4

You can almost always find a bowl of steamed broccoli, asparagus, or string beans on our dinner table, so I use the leftovers to make this salad. It's great served with a simple protein for a full meal. I like to think of it as Hot Grill Salad's (page 63) low-maintenance sister.

2 cups Brussels sprouts, trimmed and cut in half lengthwise

2 russet potatoes, peeled and roughly chopped

4 ounces baby bella mushrooms, cleaned, stems removed, and cut into halves or quarters, depending on size

1 large bunch asparagus, trimmed and cut into thirds

1 red bell pepper, cut into 1-inch squares

1 red onion, roughly chopped

1 head garlic, peeled and roughly chopped

¼ cup extra virgin olive oil

1 teaspoon fine sea salt

½ teaspoon black pepper

For a simple vinaigrette

2 garlic cloves, grated with a Microplane

3 tablespoons extra virgin olive oil

1 teaspoon Dijon mustard

2 tablespoons chopped fresh cilantro

2 tablespoons chopped fresh parsley

½ teaspoon fine sea salt

¼ teaspoon black pepper

For the arugula

½ cup arugula

Juice of ½ lemon (about 1½ tablespoons)

2 tablespoons extra virgin olive oil

½ teaspoon fine sea salt

1. Preheat the oven to 400°F and line a baking sheet with parchment paper.

2. Add the Brussels sprouts, potatoes, mushrooms, asparagus, bell pepper, onion, and garlic to a large bowl.

3. Stir in the olive oil, salt, and pepper, and use a spatula or your hands to evenly combine.

4. Transfer the veggies to the baking sheet and arrange in an even layer.

5. Roast for 40 minutes, then in the last 5 minutes increase the temperature to 500°F to help the veggies crisp up.

6. While the veggies cook, make the vinaigrette: In the same bowl you used for the veggies, whisk together the garlic, olive oil, Dijon mustard, cilantro, parsley, salt, and pepper until combined.

7. Once the veggies are crisp on the outside and tender inside, return them to the bowl and toss gently in the dressing.

8. Prepare the arugula: Just before serving, in another bowl (or just in the arugula container), dress the arugula with the lemon juice, olive oil, and salt and gently stir.

9. Plate the arugula, then top with the roasted vegetables. Serve immediately; store leftovers in an airtight container in the refrigerator for up to 3 days. Use them to pack your bowls (see page 194).

Charred Romaine

VEGETARIAN, GLUTEN-FREE

20 minutes | Serves 4 as a side

I honestly never understood the appeal of charred romaine, but then one night I found myself with a bag of romaine hearts that I didn't want to go bad. Adi was up on the roof grilling, so we threw them on, too. I was instantly converted.

This is an easy, impressive summer salad, especially when you're already preparing your meal on the grill. If you're unsure about the idea of grilling lettuce like I was, don't be. Make it and cross over to the charred romaine side with me. It's delicious here.

2 romaine hearts, halved lengthwise
3 tablespoons avocado oil
Fine sea salt and black pepper

For the tahini vinaigrette
½ cup tahini
Juice of 3 lemons (a little more than ½ cup)
3 garlic cloves, grated with a Microplane
1 teaspoon fine sea salt

1. Heat a grill (or grill pan) over medium-high heat for 5 to 10 minutes.

2. Drizzle the romaine with the avocado oil and season with salt and pepper.

3. Place the romaine, cut side down, on the grill and cook until grill marks form, 3 minutes. Carefully remove the romaine from the grill with tongs.

4. Make the tahini vinaigrette: In a small bowl, whisk the tahini and ½ cup cold water together until it's smooth and pourable. It'll get thick, then thin again, eventually reaching a perfectly smooth consistency (a bit thinner than mustard).

5. Stir in the lemon juice, garlic, and salt to combine. Taste and adjust the seasonings as needed.

6. Drizzle the romaine with the vinaigrette and serve immediately.

Hot Grill Salad

VEGETARIAN

1 hour | Serves 4 to 6

We love to entertain on our roof during warmer months. There's something about sitting around our deck table with ice-cold beverages, watching the kids play, with Adi at the grill, that makes me feel so happy and content.

When we're entertaining, the meal isn't complete without a great salad. This one keeps you out of the kitchen and allows you to stay outside with everyone and hang. You can use any veggies you love; swap the bulgur for arugula or whatever grain you've got. Make it your own—but more importantly, make this salad.

1 cup coarse bulgur

½ teaspoon fine sea salt, plus more for seasoning

1 medium zucchini, trimmed

1 red bell pepper

1 head broccoli

1 bunch asparagus, trimmed

1 garlic clove, grated

¼ cup extra virgin olive oil

2 ears of corn, shucked

Avocado oil spray

Black pepper, for seasoning

¼ cup feta

Balsamic glaze (optional)

For a simple vinaigrette

¼ cup finely chopped fresh herbs (I use a mix of chopped chives, fresh oregano, and basil)

2 tablespoons extra virgin olive oil

Juice of 1 lemon (about 3 tablespoons)

1 garlic clove, grated

½ teaspoon fine sea salt

¼ teaspoon black pepper

1. Bring 2 cups of water to a boil in a saucepan. Add the bulgur and salt. Cover and cook for 7 to 8 minutes, until the water is absorbed. Remove from the heat and set aside until you're ready to serve.

2. Preheat your grill to medium-high or heat a grill pan over medium-high heat.

3. Cut the zucchini on the bias into ½-inch slices. Cut the bell pepper into 3-inch-wide strips, and cut the broccoli lengthwise into 4 equal "steaks" (save any florets that fall off).

4. Add the cut veggies and the asparagus to a large bowl.

5. Add the grated garlic to the olive oil and whisk to combine. Pour it over the veggies and use your hands to get everything coated.

6. Grill the veggies until tender and grill marks form, 3 to 4 minutes on each side. Zucchini and asparagus cook the fastest. Season each side

continued

as you go with a pinch of salt and pepper. Transfer the grilled veggies to a large cutting board.

7. Spray the corn with avocado oil and place on the grill for 3 to 4 minutes on each side, until grill marks form.

8. While the corn cooks, make the dressing: Add the chopped herbs, olive oil, lemon juice, garlic, salt, and pepper to a large bowl and whisk to combine.

9. Once they're cool enough to handle, chop the grilled veggies and cut the corn off the cob. Add the vegetables to the dressing while warm. Stir everything together so the veggies are evenly coated in the dressing.

10. Spoon the bulgur onto a plate and add the grilled veggies on top. Crumble the feta over the veg. Adjust seasonings to taste and drizzle with balsamic glaze, if desired, for extra sweetness. Store any leftovers in an airtight container in the fridge for up to 3 days.

Grilled Chicken Salad

GLUTEN-FREE

50 minutes, not including marinating | Serves 4

Working with brands I genuinely love is one of my favorite parts about what I do. A few years ago, I worked with WeightWatchers on a partnership to create recipes and a custom pack of Baked by Melissa cupcakes. The collab was a huge success, thanks to you—I never would have been able to combine my love for cooking with cupcakes if it weren't for this incredible community.

This chicken recipe was one of the recipes I created while working with WW. It's *so* good, with the most delicious marinade. You can put the chicken on any salad. It's become one of my staples ever since.

4 boneless, skinless chicken breasts
(about 2 pounds)

For the marinade

Juice of 1 lemon (about 3 tablespoons)

1½ teaspoons fine sea salt

½ teaspoon black pepper

1 teaspoon honey

1 tablespoon dried oregano

1 teaspoon sweet paprika

1 garlic clove, grated with a Microplane

1 teaspoon garlic powder

2 tablespoons extra virgin olive oil

For the salad

5 ounces butter lettuce, chopped

4 radishes, washed and trimmed

2 to 3 scallions, trimmed

2 garlic scapes (optional)

½ cup sugar snap peas (about 15), trimmed

For the herby vinaigrette

2 tablespoons fresh parsley

2 tablespoons fresh chives

2 tablespoons fresh dill

Juice of 1 lemon (about 3 tablespoons)

1 teaspoon fine sea salt

2 tablespoons extra virgin olive oil

1 large garlic clove, grated with a Microplane

2 tablespoons white vinegar

1 teaspoon garlic powder

2 tablespoons nutritional yeast

continued

1. Place the chicken in a large Ziploc bag and pound with a mallet until it's ½ inch thick.

2. Make the marinade: Whisk together the lemon juice, salt, pepper, honey, oregano, paprika, garlic, garlic podwer, and olive oil in a small bowl. Pour the marinade into the bag with the chicken and seal, making sure to get the air out. Mix so the chicken is fully coated, and marinate in the fridge for at least 1 hour or overnight.

3. About 30 minutes before you're ready to eat, start the salad: If you marinated the chicken overnight, remove from the fridge so it can come to room temp. Add the butter lettuce to a large bowl. Use a mandoline to thinly slice the radishes and finely chop the scallions and scapes. Cut the peas into ¼-inch pieces on a bias. Add the radishes, scallions, scapes, and peas to the bowl with the lettuce.

4. Heat a frying pan over medium-high heat.

5. Make the dressing: Chop the herbs and place in a medium bowl. Whisk together the herbs, lemon juice, salt, olive oil, garlic, vinegar, garlic powder, and nutritional yeast. Set aside.

6. Place the marinated chicken on the hot pan and cook until the internal temperature reaches 165°F, 3 to 5 minutes per side.

7. Remove the chicken from the pan and transfer to a cutting board. Let rest for 5 to 10 minutes, then slice against the grain.

8. Pour the dressing over the salad and mix to evenly coat. Top with the chicken and serve immediately.

Classic Chop

GLUTEN-FREE

25 minutes | Serves 4

With a few exceptions, I'm generally not a fan of sandwiches. I find the ratio of flavors to be off—there's too much bread, making it difficult to taste all the good stuff in the middle. And what's in the middle is what I love most: the crunchy vegetables, salty salami, and creamy mozzarella. Sometimes, when I'm in the mood for more than a salad, I hollow out a baguette and stuff this salad inside. It's the best.

2 heads romaine lettuce
8 ounces fresh mozzarella
1 red bell pepper
1 cup Castelvetrano olives, pitted
½ red onion
4 to 6 slices salami

For the miso vinaigrette
⅓ cup extra virgin olive oil
Juice of 2 lemons (about ⅓ cup)
¼ cup red wine vinegar
¼ cup white miso paste
⅓ cup nutritional yeast
1 tablespoon dried oregano
2 garlic cloves, grated with a Microplane
½ teaspoon fine sea salt
Black pepper

1. Finely chop the romaine, mozzarella, bell pepper, olives, red onion, and salami and transfer to a large bowl.

2. Make the miso vinaigrette: In a small bowl, whisk together the olive oil, lemon juice, vinegar, miso, nutritional yeast, oregano, garlic, salt, and a few turns of pepper.

3. Pour dressing over the salad and mix thoroughly to combine. Serve immediately.

Smoked Tuna Soba Salad

GLUTEN-FREE*

35 minutes | Serves 4

A big salad with noodles always brings me back to the family barbecues my parents hosted when we were little. All my aunts and uncles lived a drive away, so we spent most holidays together, especially in warmer months. And there were always huge bowls of salad.

In *Come Hungry*, I included the Crunchy Ramen Slaw—a riff on a salad my mom made on repeat for these gatherings—and now we have this soba salad. I love a salad you can wrap around your fork. The ratio of veggies to noodles is very intentional: It's so you can twirl protein-heavy soba with crunchy, refreshing veggies into every bite. This is a more time-consuming salad, but it's worth every ounce of effort you put in.

½ red cabbage

1 head bok choy

2 mini cucumbers, trimmed

1 carrot, peeled

1 red bell pepper

½ cup frozen edamame

½ cup bean sprouts

¼ cup broccoli sprouts

3 scallions, light green and white parts thinly sliced

1 cup dry soba noodles

3 ounces sliced sesame-crusted smoked ahi tuna (similar to lox)

½ ripe avocado, sliced

For the miso sesame vinaigrette

Juice of 2 lemons (about ⅓ cup)

One 2-inch knob ginger, peeled

¼ cup toasted sesame oil

¼ cup avocado oil

2 tablespoons white miso paste

3 tablespoons sesame seeds

2 teaspoons tamari

1 tablespoon white vinegar

Fine sea salt and black pepper

1. Bring a large pot of water to a boil over high heat.

2. While you wait for the water to boil, use a mandoline to shred the cabbage and bok choy. When it gets close to your fingers, use a knife to finely chop the rest. Add the veggies to a large bowl.

3. Mandoline the cucumbers and carrot, then chop into thin matchsticks. Thinly slice the red bell pepper and add all the veggies to the bowl. All of the veggies should be the same thinness.

4. Run the edamame under cold water to thaw, then add it to the bowl along with the bean sprouts, broccoli sprouts, and scallions.

continued

5. Add the soba noodles to the boiling water and cook until al dente, 4 minutes. Drain the noodles and rinse with cold water to stop the cooking. Stir the noodles into the salad.

6. Make the dressing: Add the lemon juice, ginger, sesame oil, avocado oil, miso, sesame seeds, tamari, vinegar, salt, and pepper to a blender and pulse until smooth. Taste and adjust seasoning as necessary, then pour the dressing into the salad and mix well to evenly coat.

7. Transfer the salad to a large serving plate with tongs. Top with the rolled tuna (as pictured) and slices of avocado.

 Make sure to check that the soba noodles are certified GF.

How to Make a Tuna Salad

canned or jarred, water or oil—use whatever's in your pantry

tuna

canned or jarred, water or oil—use whatever's in your pantry

creamy

mayonnaise, mustard, tahini

(Tip: Use less if you use tuna in oil)

crunch

celery, carrots, bok choy

Salty bite

pickles, olives, capers

Acid

lemon juice, red wine vinegar

Flavor/ herbs

scallions, dill, parsley, cilantro, shallots, garlic

Season

salt, pepper, sweet paprika, dried herbs, garlic powder, onion powder

Tuna Salad

GLUTEN-FREE

15 minutes | Serves 3 to 4

Whenever I make tuna salad, I hear my grandmother's voice saying "tuna fish salad." She and my mom used to make it all the time for me when I was little—although I have to admit I wasn't a fan back then. Now, I totally understand the appeal. Tuna lasts in your pantry for so long, and there are so many different ways to prepare it. This method is my favorite, and if you don't have all these ingredients, that's okay. Use my guide on page 73 to make it with what you do have. Grandma, I hope you're proud.

1 to 2 leaves bok choy, cut into 1-inch pieces

1 large scallion, light green and white parts cut into 1-inch pieces

Juice of 1 lemon (about 3 tablespoons)

1½ teaspoons capers

1 medium carrot, peeled and cut into 1-inch pieces

1 teaspoon garlic powder

¼ teaspoon black pepper

1 tablespoon Dijon mustard

1 tablespoon mayonnaise

2 tablespoons fresh dill

1 teaspoon fine sea salt

2 garlic cloves, peeled

Two 6.7-ounce jars of tuna in oil

1. Add the bok choy, scallion, lemon juice, capers, carrot, garlic powder, pepper, mustard, mayonnaise, dill, salt, and garlic to the bowl of a food processor and pulse to combine.

2. Add the tuna to the food processor and pulse again until everything is well combined. Serve on toast or on a salad. Store leftovers in an airtight container in the fridge for 1 to 2 days.

 Tip If you don't have a food processor, finely chop the veggies and add all the ingredients to a large bowl. Mash well with a fork to combine.

Chicken Soup Chicken Salad

GLUTEN-FREE

15 minutes | Serves 2

I love making soup, especially in colder months. I almost always start by searing chicken in a hot pot before adding the mirepoix, like in my Chicken Broth recipe on page 101. When you return the chicken to the broth later on, it creates the most flavorful, juicy meat. It's so delicious that whenever I make soup, I save some of the shredded chicken to make this, the most incredible chicken salad you'll ever have. Sometimes, I make soup just so I can make this. It's great to pack for lunch, dip chips in, or layer inside a delicious sandwich.

1½ cups shredded chicken (ideally from Chicken Broth, page 101)

Juice of ½ lemon (about 1½ tablespoons)

1¼ teaspoon fine sea salt

¼ teaspoon black pepper

1 teaspoon garlic powder

1 celery stalk

½ pickle (I used a half sour)

3 scallions, light green and white parts

2 tablespoons chopped chives

1½ tablespoons chopped dill

1 tablespoon Dijon mustard

2 tablespoons tahini

1. Add the chicken to a large bowl (if you're using chicken from the stock recipe on page 101, add 2 or 3 tablespoons of hot stock to keep it juicy).

2. Stir the lemon juice, salt, pepper, and garlic powder into the chicken.

3. Finely chop the celery, pickle, and scallions and add to the bowl, along with the chives and dill.

4. Stir in the mustard and tahini until well combined and adjust the seasonings to taste. Serve on a sandwich, with chips, in lettuce cups, or just eat it standing over your counter. Store leftovers in an airtight container in the fridge for up to 3 days.

Green Goddess Chicken Salad

GLUTEN-FREE*

10 minutes | Serves 2 to 3

I could put this sauce in a glass and drink it. After I tasted the incredible umami flavor Better than Bouillon gave the dressing on my Cabbage Salad (page 35), I knew I had to try it in a quick Green Goddess dressing. It's different from the OG Green Goddess, but still full of nutrients. It's so vibrant, green, and packed with flavor. I blanched the spinach to keep the color bright and found that it worked really well with the leftover chicken we had in the fridge. I love this chicken salad, and I make it all the time—on a piece of sourdough toast, on its own, or in a bowl with whatever else I have in the fridge.

2 cups fresh spinach

2 garlic cloves

Juice of ½ lemon (about 1½ tablespoons)

¼ cup extra virgin olive oil

1 tablespoon seasoned vegetable base (like Better than Bouillon*) + ½ cup water or ½ cup broth

⅓ cup nutritional yeast

2 tablespoons raw, unsalted cashews

1 teaspoon fine sea salt

Black pepper

2 cups shredded chicken

Toast, to serve

1. Bring a large pot of water to a boil and set up an ice bath. Add the spinach to the boiling water and cook for 1 minute. Transfer to the ice bath to stop the cooking and let sit for 5 minutes.

2. Squeeze the excess moisture out of the spinach and add to the blender with the garlic, lemon juice, olive oil, Better than Bouillon, water, nutritional yeast, cashews, salt, and a few turns of pepper.

3. Pulse until smooth.

4. Stir the green sauce into the shredded chicken and serve on toast.

 Note To make this gluten-free, make sure to use GF-certified bouillon base.

Purple Slaw on Toast

VEGETARIAN, GLUTEN-FREE

1 hour 10 minutes, beet can be prepped in advance | Serves 2

Any beet recipe with cream reminds me of my grandpa Sammy. I have so many vivid memories of him sitting at the head of the table in my grandparents' bungalow in the Catskills, slurping a bowl of magenta borscht with a big plop of sour cream, and I'd look at it thinking it was so pretty but I'd never eat it. I thought it was so gross—and now I laugh when my kids tell me the same thing. My grandpa Sammy used to say he had a "hard bite"—meaning what exactly, we will never really know—but he'd eat tomatoes and onions in thick slices; my brother would tease him and make me laugh so hard.

That's what food is to me: memories of recipes I grew up with and cooking alongside my parents and grandparents, who shared their love of food with me. I grew up in a family where the kitchen was the center of the home, where patience was taught, and where love was shared and celebrated.

My favorite way to eat this salad is on sourdough toast, but it's also great in a bowl with other leftovers. I added the beets for color and because they make me feel amazing, and, of course, for Grandpa Sammy.

1 red beet, stem removed

1 garlic clove

Juice of ½ lemon (about 1½ tablespoons)

2 teaspoons white vinegar

1 cup cottage cheese, plus more to serve

½ teaspoon fine sea salt

¼ teaspoon black pepper

1 teaspoon garlic powder

1 small red cabbage, thinly sliced

4 slices sourdough bread, toasted

2 cups whole milk cottage cheese

Fresh herbs (I used micro cilantro)

1. Preheat the oven to 400°F and wrap the beet in aluminum foil.

2. Place the beet on a baking sheet and cook for 45 minutes to 1 hour, until tender. Remove from the oven and let cool completely.

3. Once the beet is cool, use a paper towel to remove the skin from the beet. Cut the beet in half.

4. Add half the beet, the garlic, lemon juice, vinegar, and cottage cheese to a high-powered blender and pulse until smooth. If needed, add a tablespoon or two of water to loosen it up. Add the salt, pepper, and garlic powder.

5. Thinly slice the cabbage and add it to a large bowl. Pour the dressing over the cabbage and mix to evenly coat. Serve on toast with ½ cup cottage cheese on each slice. Garnish with fresh herbs and enjoy immediately.

Green Goddess Potato Salad

VEGETARIAN, GLUTEN-FREE

30 minutes | Serves 3 as a side

Potato salad was a staple in my childhood. You know, the kind you get from a Jewish deli or diner, with a mayo-based dressing and little flecks of herbs and carrots mixed in? I'd always pick out the big chunks of potato and leave the rest.

This potato salad is nothing like the one from my childhood. It's packed with nutrients from the dill, parsley, and spinach, and it's dressed to impress, showing up as the Green Goddess herself.

1 tablespoon fine sea salt
1¼ pounds baby Yukon gold potatoes

For the ranch pesto
⅓ cup fresh dill
⅓ cup fresh parsley
⅓ cup fresh chives
1 cup spinach
1 cup grated Parmesan cheese
Juice of 1 lemon (about 3 tablespoons)
2 garlic cloves
¼ cup extra virgin olive oil
⅓ cup pine nuts
1½ teaspoons fine sea salt
½ teaspoon black pepper

1. Boil a large pot of water and season with the salt. Add the potatoes to the boiling water and cook until tender, 10 to 15 minutes.

2. Make the ranch pesto: Add the dill, parsley, chives, spinach, Parmesan, lemon juice, garlic, olive oil, and pine nuts to a food processor and pulse until smooth.

3. Scrape down the sides of the bowl and season with the salt and pepper.

4. Pulse again for about 10 seconds until everything is well combined.

5. Roughly chop the potatoes and place them in a large bowl.

6. Stir in about 1 cup of ranch pesto and serve. Store any leftovers in an airtight container in the fridge for 3 to 5 days.

Jammy Egg Salad

VEGETARIAN

15 minutes | Serves 3

Whether we were up in the Catskills visiting my grandparents or hanging around the house for a low-key weekend, egg salad was a regular in my mom and grandma's rotation. As a kid, I'd roll my eyes when my mom listed it as an option for lunch, but as I got older, I learned to appreciate this simple and versatile salad. It's easy to make and packed with protein, so it keeps you satiated until dinner.

On days when Adi and I are working from home and we've both been stuck on calls, this jammy egg salad is the perfect snack to get us through the afternoon.

6 large brown eggs
½ teaspoon fine sea salt

For serving
1 tablespoon extra virgin olive oil
3 to 4 slices sourdough bread
¼ teaspoon fine sea salt
½ teaspoon garlic powder
Fresh chives, chopped, for garnish

1. Boil a large pot of water over high heat. Carefully add the eggs to the boiling water and cook for 6 minutes 30 seconds. While the eggs cook, prepare an ice bath.

2. Transfer the cooked eggs to the ice bath with a slotted spoon.

3. Let cool for at least 5 minutes, then remove the eggs from the shells and place in a large bowl.

4. Roughly chop the eggs into small pieces against the edges of the bowl, so the soft yolks coat the whites of the egg, similar to a dressing.

5. Stir gently to combine and season with the salt.

6. To serve: Heat the olive oil in a medium frying pan over medium heat and add the bread.

7. Toast on each side until golden brown, about 3 to 4 minutes.

8. Sprinkle the bread with the salt and garlic powder. Top with the egg salad and garnish with fresh chives. Serve immediately.

Eggy Potato Salad

VEGETARIAN, GLUTEN-FREE

35 minutes | Serves 4 to 6 as a side

If you read my last cookbook, you know how much Adi's mom and family have influenced my cooking. In *Come Hungry*, there's an entire section dedicated to the salads that cover my mother-in-law's table for Shabbat dinner and family meals. This recipe is a take on one of my favorite salads she makes. Every time I eat it, I'm transported to the lawn table in her backyard in Israel. She'll serve this salad—along with so many others—in little bowls. It's a versatile, delicious salad, made extra creamy from the eggs and a pop of flavor from scallions. It's great on its own but pairs well with pretty much everything. I like to use it as a base for my meal, in the same way I'd use white rice, and add proteins or veggies right on top, mix them all together, and enjoy each and every bite.

1 tablespoon fine sea salt

1 pound (1 to 2) russet potatoes, or 1 pound baby gold potatoes (about 6)

7 eggs

For the dressing

Juice of ½ lemon (about 1½ tablespoons)

3 tablespoons mayonnaise

1 tablespoon Dijon mustard

1 teaspoon white vinegar

1 to 2 scallions, trimmed and cut into ¼-inch pieces

1 teaspoon fine sea salt

½ teaspoon black pepper

2 tablespoons chopped chives

1. Bring two large pots of water to a boil. Season one with the salt and add the potatoes; cook until tender, 10 to 15 minutes.

2. Add the eggs to the second pot of water. Cook for 11 minutes, setting up an ice bath while they cook. Transfer the eggs to the ice bath at the 11-minute mark.

3. Make the dressing: In a large bowl, whisk together the lemon juice, mayo, mustard, vinegar, scallions, salt, pepper, and chives. Once the eggs are cool, remove them from the shells and chop. Roughly chop the potatoes to be about ¾-inch cubes. Place the eggs and potatoes in the dressing and stir well to evenly coat.

4. Serve immediately, or store in an airtight container in the fridge for 3 to 5 days.

Rainbow Veggie Hummus Sandwich

VEGAN

30 minutes | Makes 1 sandwich

Yes, this is a sandwich, but it's filled with so many veggies that I think it belongs in the salad section of this cookbook. It's inspired by the Veggiewich sandwich at Lenwich, my go-to lunch spot when I'm in the office. A ton of people on social media have been ordering it, too. When I order it or make it at home, I add hummus and any other crunchy vegetable options that appeal to me. I'm more of a toast girl, as you know, so when I make a sandwich, I make sure it's stacked high with thinly sliced vegetables and protein to make it a meal. When you make this, don't skip wrapping it in parchment and tin foil to hold it together. Otherwise, it's impossible to eat.

2 slices multigrain bread

2 tablespoons hummus

1 tablespoon Dijon mustard

1 tablespoon horseradish

½ ripe avocado, sliced

¼ cup thinly sliced iceberg

2 to 3 slices ripe beefsteak tomato

Fine sea salt and black pepper

1 pickle, thinly sliced with a mandoline

1 carrot, thinly sliced with a mandoline

1 radish, thinly sliced with a mandoline

¼ cup sprouts

2 tablespoons sauerkraut

1. Place the bread slices on a piece of parchment paper, mirroring each other.

2. On one slice, spread a thick layer of hummus, and on the other, spread the mustard and horseradish in an even layer.

3. Place the avocado slices over the hummus.

4. On the side with the horseradish, layer the iceberg and tomatoes, then season with salt and pepper. Add the pickle over the avocado, followed by the carrot, radish, sprouts, and sauerkraut.

5. Stack the tomato side over the other and fold the parchment paper to keep everything inside. Cut in half to serve; enjoy immediately.

Taco Salad Nachos

GLUTEN-FREE, VEGETARIAN*

1 hour 15 minutes | Serves 4 to 6

I'm the girl who digs to find the perfect bite of whatever it is I'm indulging in. With nachos, I go for the pieces with lots of gooey melted cheese, then use the remaining chips to scoop up all the veggies I can find—all to create the perfect bite.

That can take work, so I created a recipe that makes it easier for everyone to get the perfect ratio of flavors, no digging required. By loading the nachos with salad, every cheese-covered chip becomes a delicious vessel, just how I like it. This is a great snack to make for the Super Bowl—you can make the salad on the side ahead of time, then put it all together when you're ready to serve. It's a crowd-pleaser, and a great way to take something everyone already knows and loves to the next level.

For the shredded chicken

1 cup bone broth

2 teaspoons sweet paprika

1 teaspoon fine sea salt

¼ teaspoon black pepper

1 teaspoon ground turmeric

1 teaspoon seasoned vegetable base (like Better than Bouillon*)

3 garlic cloves, grated with a Microplane

Juice of ½ lemon (1½ tablespoons)

3 boneless, skinless chicken breasts (about 1½ pounds)

For the taco salad nachos

1 head iceberg lettuce

1 red bell pepper

1 bunch scallions

1 cup cherry tomatoes

2 garlic cloves, grated with a Microplane

½ teaspoon fine sea salt

¼ teaspoon black pepper

1 teaspoon sweet paprika

6 ounces Gruyère cheese (about 2 cups shredded)

8 ounces sharp cheddar (about 2 cups shredded)

9-ounce bag tortilla chips*

2 ripe avocados, sliced

1 cup sour cream

¼ cup chopped parsley

For a simple vinaigrette

Juice of 2 lemons (about ⅓ cup)

⅓ cup extra virgin olive oil

½ teaspoon fine sea salt

1 tablespoon rice vinegar

1 garlic clove, grated with a Microplane

continued

1. Make the chicken: Whisk together the bone broth, paprika, salt, pepper, turmeric, vegetable base, grated garlic, and lemon juice in a medium saucepan.

2. Place the chicken in the pot and make sure it's fully submerged in liquid. If it's not fully covered, add water until the chicken is submerged.

3. Place the pot over medium-high heat and bring to a simmer (it should take about 3 minutes).

4. Lower the heat and cover the pot. Cook until the internal temperature of the chicken reaches 165°F, 25 to 30 minutes.

5. Transfer the chicken from the pot to a stand mixer fitted with the paddle attachment and add a few tablespoons of the poaching liquid. Start with the mixer on low, then gradually increase the speed as the chicken shreds. Don't start too fast or you'll get splashed. Once the chicken is completely shredded (it should take less than a minute), add another few tablespoons of the poaching liquid and set aside.

6. While the chicken cooks, prepare the nachos: Cut the iceberg into thin ribbons and place in a large bowl. You should end up with about 8 cups. Finely chop the red pepper and light green and white parts of the scallions and add to the bowl.

7. Cut the tomatoes in half lengthwise then into thirds and place in a separate small bowl. Add the garlic cloves, salt, pepper, and sweet paprika over the tomatoes and stir to combine.

8. Make the vinaigrette: In a small bowl, whisk together the lemon juice, olive oil, salt, vinegar, and garlic until combined.

9. Preheat the oven to 450°F.

10. Shred the cheese with a box grater.

11. Arrange a thin layer of tortilla chips on a quarter sheet pan and cover with the grated cheese and shredded chicken. Add another layer of chips, creating a well in the middle, and top with more cheese and chicken.

12. Place the pan in the oven for 5 to 6 minutes to melt the cheese. Keep an eye on it so it doesn't burn.

13. When the cheese has melted, remove the pan from the oven. Pour the dressing over the iceberg mixture and mix to combine. Spread the salad over the chips in an even layer and top with the tomatoes. Save extra salad to replenish as it gets eaten off the nachos.

14. Top with the sliced avocado, sour cream, and parsley.

 Tip To make the sour cream the perfect pourable consistency, add a squeeze of lemon juice.

 Note Make sure to check that the seasoned vegetable base and tortilla chips you use are certified GF. Skip the chicken to make it vegetarian.

soup

I was raised by women who prescribed soup to cure a cold, but the soups I grew up eating were not very filling or exciting—like chicken soup or matzo ball soup (which is also chicken soup). They were also most often eaten as the predecessor to a meal, not a meal itself, so I never really understood the point of it all. And when I just had soup, I'd be hungry an hour later. It wasn't until I got older and started to cook for myself that I realized how incredible it could be. The brothy nature of soup provides the perfect blank canvas to create a meal that warms you up and gives you the perfect balance of slurp and chew.

The soups you'll find here are hearty—the kind you can enjoy as a meal. This is because I believe that if you're going to put the time in, you should come out of it feeling full. There are no soups here that will leave you feeling hungry an hour after you eat it. These recipes are filled with delicious, nourishing ingredients that will make you feel great, because in my book, that's the only way to do soup.

Bone Broth

GLUTEN-FREE

6 hours 45 minutes | Makes 8 cups

Bone broth is a project. It's something you do on a snowy weekend when you have no plans. Time is an ingredient, and with bone broth, when you've got the time, there's no better activity. The end result is a gift you give yourself and the people you share it with. Bone broth is rich, delicious, and comforting, and taking the time to make it during a cold winter weekend and freezing the result creates a soul-warming base for soups in the weeks and months to come.

You can use any bones you want or have on hand for this. The time and attention you give are what create magic. You'll taste the love in every sip.

2 large carrots

2 celery stalks

1 onion

2 heads garlic

3 to 4 large bones—leftover T-bone from a porterhouse steak, shoulder bones, oxtail, etc.

3 tablespoons extra virgin olive oil

1 teaspoon whole peppercorns

3 to 4 bay leaves

Fine sea salt and black pepper

1. Preheat the oven to 450°F and line a baking sheet with parchment paper. Trim the carrots and celery, cut the onion in half, and cut the bottoms off the garlic.

2. Place the bones in a large pot and cover with water. Bring to a boil, then lower the heat to a simmer. Cook for 15 minutes. This step removes the impurities from the bones! This isn't your broth yet.

3. Remove the bones from the pot and dry them off. Discard the water. Place the bones on the prepared baking sheet with the vegetables. Cover everything with the olive oil.

4. Roast for 30 minutes, until the bones are brown and the veggies are soft and slightly golden. Add all of the veggies and bones into a large stockpot and cover with water.

5. Add the peppercorns and bay leaves to the pot and set over high heat.

continued

6. Bring the water to a boil then reduce heat to a simmer. Cover the pot and cook for 4 to 6 hours. Use a large spoon or ladle to skim the fat off the surface.

7. Strain the vegetables and bone out of the pot carefully over a bowl large enough to hold all the broth.

8. Season the broth to taste with salt and pepper and place in a freezer-safe container. Store in the refrigerator for up to 5 days or freeze for up to 3 months. When the broth is cold, any remaining fat will solidify at the top, and you can simply remove with a spoon before cooking. Save to use in soups, stews, or other cooking.

- Freeze leftover bones from steaks and stews to make broth, and stock up on them (pun intended) from the market or butcher. They're typically inexpensive.
- Roast the bones with veggies to bring out extra flavor before simmering.
- Simmer, covered, for at least 24 hours—turning the heat off while you sleep—to make sure the broth is infused with every nutrient. Covering the pan will also create a more gelatinous end result.
- Salt the broth at the end to taste and add a squeeze of lemon juice to cut the richness.
- After straining the broth, use a ladle or slotted spoon to skim the fat off the top. Chill the broth, then remove any layer of fat that has risen to the top. When the broth is cold, this should come off easily.

Chicken Broth

GLUTEN-FREE

4 hours | Makes 8 cups

Homemade broths can be intimidating, I get it. We're here to conquer your fears. Let's do it together.

It's so easy to buy broth at the store or have it delivered with your groceries. And honestly, I'm not telling you to stop doing that. I always recommend having stock on hand. There are also times when making homemade broth will completely transform your dish, become a vessel for you to deliver your love, or to let people know how much they mean to you. Meeting your future in-laws for the first time or hosting people for holiday meals are two such occasions. (Pro tip: For those special occasions, you should make the broth before those meals and freeze it—don't make yourself crazy on an already stressful day.)

If you're like me and love to futz around in the kitchen, chopping and cooking and lifting the pot lid to smell what's inside, you should make your own broth. The longer it cooks, the better it becomes—it's a great base, rich in flavor and nutrients.

It's time. We're in it together, remember?

1 tablespoon avocado oil

One 4- to 6-pound chicken, giblets removed

2 onions, cut in half

3 or 4 celery stalks, cut into 2-inch pieces

2 or 3 carrots, cut into 1-inch pieces

2 bay leaves

½ teaspoon whole peppercorns

1. Heat the avocado oil in a large stockpot over medium heat. Once shimmering, add the chicken.

2. Cook until golden brown on one side, 5 to 7 minutes. Use tongs to flip and sear on the other side. Cook for 5 to 7 minutes more, then remove the chicken from the pot.

3. Add the onions (cut side down), celery, and carrots to the pot. Cook until the bottom of the onions are golden, just a few minutes, then return the chicken to the pot and cover everything with fresh water by 2 inches.

4. Raise the heat to high and add the bay leaves and peppercorns. Bring to a boil, then lower the heat to a simmer and cover.

continued

5. Cook for 1 hour 30 minutes, then remove the chicken from the pot and shred the meat. Reserve 1½ cups of chicken to make Chicken Soup Chicken Salad (page 77), and return the bones to the pot.

6. Continue to cook the broth over low heat, covered, for as long as you can, up to 3 hours.

7. When the broth is deep golden, place a large bowl in the sink and set a fine-mesh strainer inside. Carefully drain the liquid into the pot so none of it goes down the drain. If there's a lot of sediment, line the strainer with cheesecloth and strain carefully once more.

8. Store the chicken broth in the freezer in an airtight container for up to 2 months. Use to make soup or in other recipes.

Quick Veggie Soup

VEGAN

35 minutes | Serves 4 to 6

This is my trick for making a hearty soup really quickly using ingredients you already have on hand. Vegetable (or chicken) broth is one of my kitchen staples—we always have a supply in our freezer, pantry, or storage area. Sometimes all three!

I'm giving you my go-to quick soup recipe here but want you to make it your own. Every soup I make starts with a mirepoix: onions, carrots, and celery. If you don't have all three, that's okay. Shallots work instead of onions (here, it's a leek). Then throw in a can of beans, whatever leftover veggies you have in your fridge, a grain if you want, some herbs, and in no time, and with very little effort, you'll have a delicious soup that makes you feel good.

2 leeks

1 large carrot, peeled

1 tablespoon avocado oil

½ teaspoon fine sea salt, plus more to taste

Black pepper

6 cups vegetable broth

One 15-ounce can cannellini beans

One 15-ounce can chickpeas

1 large head bok choy

3 garlic cloves, grated with a Microplane

⅓ cup bulgur

1 medium zucchini

1 bunch broccolini or 1 head broccoli

⅓ cup chopped fresh parsley

Juice of 1 lemon cheek (about 2 teaspoons)

2 teaspoons za'atar

1. Trim and clean the leeks, then cut into ½-inch pieces. (You may need to rinse them again in a colander or salad spinner if they're very sandy.) Cut the carrot into ½-inch coins.

2. Heat the avocado oil in a large pot over medium heat and add the leek and carrot. Season with ¼ teaspoon of the salt and a few turns of pepper.

3. Cook the veggies until the leeks are soft, about 5 to 7 minutes, then add the broth and bring to a boil.

4. Meanwhile, rinse and drain the beans and chickpeas, then add them to the pot.

5. Trim and wash the bok choy, then cut into ¼-inch pieces. Add them to the pot.

continued

6. Add the garlic to the soup along with the bulgur. Bring the soup to a boil.

7. Cut the zucchini into ½-inch half moons and the broccolini into ½-inch florets. Add them to the soup once it's boiling and you're about 5 minutes away from serving. Stir in the parsley.

8. Squeeze the lemon juice into the pot, then add the za'atar. Season with remaining ¼ teaspoon salt and a few more turns of pepper, then adjust the seasonings as needed. Store leftovers in an airtight container in the fridge for up to 4 days, or freeze for up to 3 months.

Green Tofu Noodle Soup

VEGAN, GLUTEN-FREE

45 minutes | Serves 4 to 6

This is one of my favorite soups. It's deceptively easy, given how beautiful the output is. In the past few years, I've started marinating the tofu in ginger, tamari, and toasted sesame oil, which adds so much flavor, and added the herby garnish for an extra pop of color. I love a soup that has all the elements of a meal (green, grain, protein) because it makes the effort worth it.

1 tablespoon avocado oil

3 shallots, sliced

2 cups chopped mushrooms
use a mix of shiitake, oyster, and brown beech

5 to 7 garlic cloves, chopped

Fine sea salt and black pepper

4 cups vegetable broth

4 cups water

2 bunches bok choy

1 small head broccoli

1 cup sugar snap peas

2.1 ounces rice noodles

For the tofu

One 14-ounce block extra-firm tofu

1 tablespoon minced ginger

¼ cup tamari

2 tablespoons toasted sesame oil

2 garlic cloves, grated

2 tablespoons white miso paste

For the topping

½ cup chopped herbs (a mix of parsley and cilantro)

2 scallions, light green and white parts cut into ¼-inch pieces

1 teaspoon sesame seeds

¼ teaspoon fine sea salt

Black pepper

1. Heat the avocado oil in a large pot over medium heat. Add the shallots and cook for 5 to 7 minutes, stirring occasionally, until translucent.

2. Add the mushrooms and cook for 3 to 5 minutes, until soft. Stir in the garlic and cook for 1 to 2 minutes, until aromatic. Season with salt and a few turns of pepper.

3. Pour in the broth and water and bring to a simmer.

4. While the soup cooks, press the tofu with a tea towel to get excess liquid out and cut into ½-inch cubes.

5. Whisk together the ginger, tamari, sesame oil, garlic, and miso in a medium bowl and add the tofu. Stir gently to cover the tofu with the sauce, then let sit for about 10 minutes.

6. Thinly slice the bok choy and finely chop the broccoli and peas. Add all the veggies and the rice noodles to the pot.

7. Stir in the tofu and additional sauce and cook for 10 minutes.

8. While the noodles and tofu cook, make the topping. In a small bowl, combine the herbs, scallions, sesame seeds, salt, and a few turns of pepper.

9. Taste the soup and adjust seasonings as needed (the tamari will add salt, so it depends what kind you use). Garnish with a spoonful of the topping and serve immediately.

Squash Soup

VEGAN

45 minutes | Serves 4

Most squash soup looks (and tastes) like baby food to me. So I added breadcrumbs, kept in a few whole veggies, and created a soup that surprised me—it became one of my favorites. It's an easy-to-throw-together meal, perfect if you're new to the soup game.

3 tablespoons extra virgin olive oil

3 celery stalks, chopped

1 large carrot, cut into coins

1 yellow onion, chopped

Fine sea salt and black pepper

2 Yukon gold potatoes, chopped

8 garlic cloves, chopped

4 cups vegetable broth

1 bay leaf

1 teaspoon cumin

1 teaspoon garlic powder

1 koginut squash, peeled and cut into 1-inch pieces

1 medium zucchini, chopped

For the topping

2 garlic cloves, grated with a Microplane

2 tablespoons extra virgin olive oil

1 cup breadcrumbs

2 tablespoons chopped fresh parsley

1. Heat the olive oil in a stockpot set over medium heat and add the celery, carrot, and onion.

2. Season the veggies with ½ teaspoon salt and a few turns of pepper. Cook until the vegetables soften, 7 to 10 minutes.

3. Add the potatoes and garlic to the pot and cook until fragrant, a few minutes more.

4. Pour in the vegetable broth and 4 cups of water. Stir in the bay leaf, cumin, and garlic powder and bring to a boil.

5. Lower the heat and simmer for 10 minutes. Remove the bay leaf and blend the soup with an immersion blender until smooth.

6. Add the squash and zucchini and cook until soft, but not overcooked, about 15 minutes. Taste and adjust the seasonings as needed.

7. Make the topping: Add the garlic and olive oil to a medium skillet over medium heat. Add the breadcrumbs. Toss occasionally, so the breadcrumbs don't burn, and cook until the breadcrumbs are toasted, about 3 to 4 minutes.

8. Stir the parsley into the toasted breadcrumbs. Top the soup with the breadcrumb topping just before serving (or let everyone top their own). Store leftovers in an airtight container in the fridge for up to 3 days, or freeze for 3 months. Keep the breadcrumb topping separate.

Creamy Tomato Soup

VEGAN, GLUTEN-FREE

1 hour | Serves 4

Tomato season is the best time of year, and when I spot them at my local farmers market, I always buy more than I need. I get so excited. I'd like to say this only happens on my first few trips to the market, but it happens every time I spot perfectly red, hard tomatoes. I keep them in bowls on my kitchen counter so they're top of mind until they're transformed into a delicious soup, salad, or toast topping.

This soup is a staple in our house when tomatoes are at their best. I love to use the leftovers as if it were tomato sauce on my kids' pasta—it makes me feel so good about myself when they slurp it up. And it's creamy! You'd never know it's vegan.

12 Roma tomatoes
1 head garlic, peeled
1 yellow onion, cut in half
⅓ cup extra virgin olive oil, plus more to serve
½ teaspoon fine sea salt
¼ teaspoon black pepper
1 teaspoon garlic powder
1 teaspoon dried oregano
1 teaspoon fresh rosemary
1 teaspoon fresh thyme, plus more to serve
4 cups vegetable broth, plus more as needed
¼ cup coconut cream, plus more to serve

1. Preheat the oven to 400°F.

2. Quarter the tomatoes and place them in a shallow casserole dish with the garlic, onion, olive oil, salt, and pepper. Stir to evenly coat the vegetables.

3. Bake for 30 minutes, until the tomatoes are tender and start to brown slightly.

4. Stir in the garlic powder, oregano, rosemary, and thyme while the tomatoes are still hot.

5. Transfer the veggies to a blender along with the vegetable broth and coconut cream and purée until smooth. Taste and adjust the seasonings as needed. You can also add more broth to thin it out if you prefer.

6. Top with a drizzle of olive oil and coconut cream and serve immediately. Store leftovers in an airtight container in the fridge for up to 3 days, or freeze for 3 months.

Tortellini Soup

VEGETARIAN

45 minutes | Serves 4

My parents picked up my kids from school the day I made this, so I sent them home with a deli container filled with soup. The next day, my dad texted asking for the recipe. They loved it. It's the perfect balance of tortellini to broth. I would get a stomachache if I ate a big bowl of tortellini and sauce, but this gives me the same flavor plus a little bit of greens.

1 tablespoon avocado oil

1 yellow onion, chopped

3 carrots, peeled and chopped

7 garlic cloves, roughly chopped

1 teaspoon fine sea salt, plus more to taste

Black pepper

1 pint cherry or grape tomatoes

4 cups vegetable broth, plus more as needed

½ cup freshly grated Parmesan cheese, plus more to serve

1 teaspoon sweet paprika

1 teaspoon dried oregano

9 ounces fresh four-cheese tortellini

1 bunch broccolini, chopped

1. Heat the avocado oil in a large stockpot over medium-high heat and add the onion. Cook until nearly translucent, 5 to 7 minutes. Add the carrots and cook until slightly softened, 3 to 5 minutes more.

2. Add the garlic to the pot and cook until fragrant, about 1 minute. Season with ¼ teaspoon of the salt and a few turns of pepper.

3. Add the tomatoes to the pot, breaking them up with the back of a wooden spoon as they burst, 5 minutes. Once they're mostly softened, pour in the broth and 1 cup water. Cover the pot and bring to a boil.

4. Once the liquid boils, remove the pot from heat. The tomatoes should be completely soft. Use an immersion or high-powered blender to blend the soup until smooth. If you use a traditional blender, keep the hole in the lid open but covered with a kitchen towel so it doesn't explode when you take the lid off. Add additional broth or water to thin it out, if desired.

5. Return the soup to the pot (if you used a traditional blender) over medium-low heat.

6. Stir in the Parmesan, paprika, oregano, and remaining ¾ teaspoon salt, then add the tortellini and broccolini. Cook until the tortellini is tender, 5 to 7 minutes. Taste and adjust seasonings as needed.

Marak Couscous

VEGAN

45 minutes | Serves 4

In Hebrew, "marak couscous" translates to couscous soup. I can't think of it without hearing my mother-in-law's voice asking if we want to eat it. The answer is always *yes*—it's a celebration of vegetables served over a bed of couscous, filled with broth. It's soul food. I feel a huge sense of responsibility to my mother-in-law whenever I make it, and I always ask Adi if I'm doing it right (he wants me to tell you that he makes it, too). Whatever you do, always plate the couscous before adding the soup to the bowl, then season to taste. Any other way to make it would be a crime. I love you, Tata. Thank you for sharing your recipe with me.

1 cup couscous (Moroccan-style, not pearl or Israeli)

2 tablespoons plus 1 teaspoon extra virgin olive oil

1½ teaspoons fine sea salt

1 large yellow onion, chopped

3 celery stalks

½ head green cabbage

2 large carrots, peeled

2 russet potatoes, peeled

1 sweet potato, peeled

1 butternut squash, peeled

Black pepper

4 cups vegetable broth

1½ teaspoons ground turmeric

2 bay leaves

One 15-ounce can chickpeas, drained and rinsed

1 medium zucchini, trimmed

Juice of ½ lemon (1½ tablespoons)

Parsley, to serve

1. Bring ½ cup water to a boil in a small pot. Stir in the couscous, 1 teaspoon of the olive oil, and ½ teaspoon of the salt and cover the pot. Remove from the heat and let stand for 5 minutes.

2. Uncover the pot and fluff the couscous with a fork. The liquid should be fully absorbed.

3. Heat the remaining 2 tablespoons olive oil in a stockpot over medium heat and add the onion. Cook until translucent, 5 to 7 minutes.

4. While the onion cooks, cut the celery, cabbage, carrots, russet potatoes, sweet potato, and squash into 1-inch pieces.

5. Season the onion with ½ teaspoon of the salt and a few turns of pepper.

6. Add the celery to the pot and cook for a few minutes, then add the cabbage and carrots.

continued

7. Season the potatoes and squash with the remaining ½ teaspoon salt and a few more turns of pepper and add to the pot. Stir to combine.

8. Pour the broth and 4 cups of water into the pot with the turmeric and bay leaves. Bring to a boil, then add the chickpeas.

9. Cut the zucchini into ½-inch rounds and then into quarters. Add them to the pot and let simmer until softened, 10 to 15 minutes.

10. Remove the soup from heat and fish out the bay leaves with a wooden spoon. Squeeze in the lemon juice just before serving. Finely chop the parsley.

11. Scoop ¼ cup to ½ cup couscous into each bowl, then pour the soup over. Garnish with parsley and serve immediately. Store leftover soup and couscous separately in airtight containers in the fridge for up to 4 days.

Lentil Soup

VEGAN, GLUTEN-FREE

1 hour | Serves 4

This is a great first soup to make if you're new to the soup game or learning how to cook, because it's hard to mess up. Adi likes the taste of lentils more than I do, but I love how good they are for you. They're really high in protein, fiber, iron, and other nutrients. I like my lentil soup on the creamier side, and the longer you cook this, the creamier it becomes. Adi prefers his lentils al dente and his soup thick, and that's what this recipe gives you. I'd be lying if I told you this is one of my favorite recipes, because it isn't, but it's one of Adi's and I make it with him in mind. Add more broth and simmer longer to adjust it to your personal preferences. Serve without croutons to keep it gluten free.

3 tablespoons extra virgin olive oil

1 yellow onion, finely chopped

1 large shallot, finely chopped

2 carrots, finely chopped

3 celery stalks, finely chopped

10 garlic cloves, finely chopped

1 teaspoon fine sea salt, plus more to taste

½ teaspoon black pepper, plus more to taste

2 cups sprouted lentils

2 teaspoons garlic powder

2 teaspoons sweet paprika

1 teaspoon onion powder

4 cups vegetable broth

For the croutons (optional)

¼ cup extra virgin olive oil

2 garlic cloves, grated

4 slices sourdough bread

½ teaspoon fine sea salt

1. Heat the olive oil in a large pot over medium heat. Add the onion, shallot, carrots, and celery and cook until the onions are translucent, 5 to 7 minutes.

2. Stir in the garlic and cook until aromatic, about 1 minute.

3. Add the salt and pepper, then add the sprouted lentils.

4. Stir in the garlic powder, sweet paprika, and onion powder and toast for 1 minute.

5. Pour in the broth and bring to a boil.

6. Cover and let simmer for 30 minutes to an hour, or until you're ready to serve. Season to taste.

7. If you are making the croutons: Heat the olive oil in a large skillet over medium heat and add the garlic. Cut the bread into ¾-inch cubes and add them to the pan.

8. Toast the bread on all sides until golden brown, 3 to 5 minutes on either side, then season with the salt.

9. Top the soup with croutons just before serving. Store any leftovers in an airtight container in the fridge for up to 4 days, or in the freezer for up to 3 months.

Carrot Ginger Soup

VEGAN, GLUTEN-FREE

1 hour 15 minutes | Serves 4 to 6

I first made this soup for a close friend who needed some love and healing. Fresh ginger and turmeric are the stars of this recipe, and I wanted to make sure their flavors packed a punch. I also find ginger incredibly difficult to grate by hand and if you've ever cooked with turmeric root, you know that it dyes anything it touches yellow. So, instead of grating or chopping, I blend them together with broth to create a rich, vibrant liquid that goes right into the soup. You can use this method for any recipe that uses ginger and turmeric. It's a great shortcut (and so good for you).

2 small yellow onions

3 celery stalks

6 medium carrots

2 tablespoons avocado oil

1 teaspoon fine sea salt, plus more as needed

1 medium sweet potato, peeled

6 cups vegetable broth

One 3-inch knob fresh ginger or 3 tablespoons ginger paste

One 3-inch knob fresh turmeric root or 1 tablespoon ground turmeric

One 15-ounce can chickpeas, drained and rinsed

1 cup red lentils, rinsed

½ cup coconut milk

1½ teaspoons cumin

¼ teaspoon black pepper, plus more as needed

1. Chop the onions and celery and cut the carrots into ½-inch-thick coins.

2. Heat the avocado oil in a large stockpot and add the veggies. Season with ¼ teaspoon of the salt.

3. While the vegetables cook, roughly chop the sweet potato into ½-inch-thick cubes, then add to the pot. Stir to combine.

4. Pour in the broth and cover with a lid to bring to a simmer.

5. While the soup cooks, peel the ginger and turmeric and add to a blender. Scoop out about a cup of broth from the soup and add to the blender; pulse until completely smooth.

6. Pour the ginger-turmeric mixture into the soup, and add the chickpeas and lentils.

7. Bring the soup to a boil, then lower the heat to a simmer. Continue cooking until the veggies are soft and the lentils are tender, about 1 hour.

8. Stir in the coconut milk, cumin, remaining ¾ teaspoon salt, and the pepper. Adjust the seasonings to taste and serve. Store leftovers in an airtight container in the fridge for up to 3 days, or freeze for up to 3 months.

Healing Chicken Soup

DAIRY-FREE, GLUTEN-FREE

1 hour | Serves 5

It's funny that I have so many chicken soup recipes in this book, because as a kid, I never wanted the chicken soup my mom made. I'm sure she thinks it's ironic, too. Chicken soup is healing—she used to call it "Jewish penicillin," in a thick Queens accent that my brother and I sometimes teased her for.

The women in my family are all *balaboostas*—women who nourish their families with delicious, vibrant recipes. And all of them, from my mom to my grandmothers Annie and Sylvia, made chicken soup to care for their families. When I became a mom, I suddenly wanted to make chicken soup, too. Of all my chicken soups, this is one I return to again and again, because it's packed with anti-inflammatory ingredients like ginger and turmeric, which also add incredible flavor. I love to make it for my friends when they're sick. I keep one deli container for myself and bring the rest to them. It's better than anything you could order to be delivered—this soup gives friends your time, effort, and love. And you can taste it in every healing bite.

2 tablespoons extra virgin olive oil

1 large yellow onion, chopped

1 large carrot, peeled

1 head garlic, peeled and roughly chopped, plus 3 cloves

1 teaspoon fine sea salt, plus more to taste

½ teaspoon black pepper, plus more to taste

4 bone-in, skin-on chicken thighs

½ cup white rice

1½-inch knob fresh ginger, grated

1 teaspoon ground turmeric

3 cups vegetable broth

3 cups bone broth

1 lemon, cut in half

¼ cup coconut milk

1. Heat the olive oil in a large pot over medium heat. Add the onion and cook until translucent, 5 to 7 minutes.

2. Roughly chop the carrot and add it to the pot with the onion. Cook until the vegetables have softened, another 5 to 7 minutes. Add the roughly chopped garlic.

3. Season with ½ teaspoon of the salt and the pepper. Push the veggies to the side with your spoon to make room on the bottom of the pot for the chicken.

4. Pat the chicken thighs dry and add to the pot, skin side down.

continued

5. Add the rice, ginger, and turmeric, and stir to combine.

6. Pour in the vegetable broth and bone broth (you can do all vegetable or all bone broth, or a combination).

7. Squeeze half the lemon into the pot and throw it in.

8. Lower the heat to a simmer and cook for 30 to 40 minutes, until the chicken is fully cooked and the rice is tender..

9. Remove the chicken from the pot. Let cool slightly, then shred using two forks. Return the shredded chicken to the pot.

10. Add the remaining ½ teaspoon salt and adjust seasonings to taste.

11. Grate the remaining 3 garlic cloves directly into the pot and stir.

12. Taste the soup and squeeze the other half of the lemon in.

13. Stir in the coconut milk and season with more pepper. Serve immediately.

14. Store any leftovers in an airtight container in the fridge for up to 4 days, or in the freezer for up to 3 months.

Creamy Chicken Soup

GLUTEN-FREE, DAIRY-FREE

1 hour | Serves 6

This recipe was inspired by Greek avgolemono. When we first started Baked by Melissa, after a long day of work, my parents, my brother, and I would all go to Taverna Kyclades at Fourteenth Street and First Avenue, an incredible Greek restaurant a few blocks from our first store. They didn't take reservations, but the delicious lemon potatoes and creamy avgolemono soup were worth the wait. My version, like theirs, is made creamy thanks to eggs whisked with hot broth, but it veers from tradition with the addition of ginger and turmeric.

This rich, creamy soup doesn't include dairy, and has extra protein. Every soup in this book is designed to leave you feeling full and nourished, because if you're going to all the trouble to make a soup, you should feel fulfilled when you eat it. And this is one of my favorites.

4 boneless, skin-on chicken thighs (about 1 pound)

1 teaspoon fine sea salt

2 yellow onions, trimmed and peeled

3 celery stalks, trimmed

3 medium carrots, trimmed and peeled

6 to 8 garlic cloves, roughly chopped

Black pepper

8 cups vegetable broth

½ cup white rice

¾ tablespoon grated ginger

2 teaspoons turmeric

2 eggs

Juice of 1 lemon (about 3 tablespoons)

Scallions, thinly sliced, to garnish

1. Heat a large stockpot over medium heat. While it heats up, pat dry the chicken with paper towels and season with ½ teaspoon of the salt. Add the chicken to the pot, skin-side down, to sear.

2. After about 3 minutes, flip the chicken to sear the other side.

3. While the chicken cooks, roughly chop the onions, celery, and carrots.

4. Remove the chicken from the pot and add the veggies, stirring to scrape up any brown bits that may have stuck to the bottom of the pot.

5. Cook until the onions are translucent, stirring occasionally, 5 to 7 minutes. Stir in the garlic and season with the remaining ½ teaspoon salt and a few turns of pepper.

continued

6. Cook the garlic until aromatic, 1 to 2 minutes. Pour in the vegetable broth, then return the chicken to the pot. Cover and bring to a boil.

7. Lower the heat to a simmer and cook for 45 minutes to let the flavors come together. Stir in the rice, ginger, and turmeric, and remove the chicken from the pot.

8. Shred the chicken and return the meat to the soup.

9. In a medium bowl, whisk together the eggs and lemon juice.

10. Slowly, *slowly*, whisk 2 cups of broth from the soup into the bowl with the eggs to temper the egg mixture. It's really important to add the broth to the eggs in a slow, steady stream so the eggs don't scramble.

11. Add the egg mixture to the soup slowly (about ½ cup at a time), stirring as you go.

12. Remove the soup from heat and garnish with scallions. Serve immediately.

Leeky Chicken Soup

GLUTEN-FREE

1 hour 30 minutes | Serves 4

"OMG, I have a leek!"

I love leeks, for entertainment and for eating. They're a milder, softer onion, and are in peak season from November to March (conveniently, soup season). The longer you cook leeks, the more they melt in your mouth. I like to make this soup with chicken thighs, because we always have them in our freezer, and more often than not I'll throw in a cup of leftover rice we have in the fridge from dinner the night before. It's so easy. Add a few herbs on top if you have them to make it beautiful, then slurp it all up.

3 leeks, trimmed and washed thoroughly

1 large yellow onion

2 large carrots

4 bone-in, skin-on chicken thighs (about 1½ pounds)

1 teaspoon fine sea salt, plus more to season

1 teaspoon black pepper, plus more to season

2 tablespoons extra virgin olive oil

12 garlic cloves

2 teaspoons oregano

1 teaspoon garlic powder

2 cups chicken or vegetable broth (use what you have)

1 cup cooked rice or ½ cup uncooked rice

1 lemon cheek

Fresh dill and chives, to garnish

1. Cut the leeks in half lengthwise, then chop into ¼-inch pieces. Roughly chop the onion. Cut the carrots into ½-inch coins.

2. Season each chicken leg with ¼ teaspoon each of salt and pepper.

3. Heat the olive oil in a large pot over medium heat. Once shimmering, add the chicken thighs, skin-side down. Once they're in the pot, season the reverse side.

4. Sear the chicken until the skin is golden, 3 minutes per side.

5. Remove the chicken from the pot and add the leeks, onion, and carrots, stirring occasionally, until the onions begin to caramelize, about 10 minutes.

6. While the veggies cook, roughly chop 10 garlic cloves.

7. Stir the garlic into the pot and cook until fragrant, 1 minute.

8. Add the salt, oregano, garlic powder, and a few turns of pepper.

continued

9. Pour in the broth and 2 cups water and stir to combine.

10. Return the chicken to the pot. Cover and bring to a boil, then lower the heat. Simmer for 1 hour, until the flavors meld.

11. Remove the chicken thighs from the soup and shred the chicken. Return the meat to the pot.

12. Add the cooked rice and cook over low heat for 20 minutes more. (You can also use uncooked rice; add ½ cup when you add the shredded chicken.)

13. Once the rice is tender, squeeze the lemon cheek into the pot and grate the remaining 2 garlic cloves with a Microplane directly into the soup. Adjust the seasonings to taste.

14. Garnish with dill, chives, or any other herbs you have and love. Store any leftovers in an airtight container in the fridge for up to 4 days, or in the freezer for up to 3 months.

Cheater Chicken Soup

DAIRY-FREE

1 hour 15 minutes | Serves 4

You're not cheating if you make this soup. You're actually beating the system. I really enjoy the process of making a slow-cooked soup, where you start with a whole chicken and let it cook all day long to create an incredible broth. But you can also get great-quality broth at the store—often in the freezer section—and let it do all the work for you. Once you have good stock, go to your pantry, see what you have, and throw it all into a pot. All soups require a few key ingredients: mirepoix (onions, carrots, celery), protein (a can of beans, chicken), and veggies. You can add a grain if you want, but it's not necessary. Instead of the slow-simmered chicken soup that used to take me a day to make, this is the soup I crave now. It's incredible.

2 whole chicken legs (about 1 pound)

1¼ teaspoons fine sea salt, plus more to taste

½ teaspoon black pepper, plus more to taste

Avocado oil spray

3 carrots, peeled

1 yellow onion

3 to 4 celery stalks

6 to 8 garlic cloves, roughly chopped

4 cups chicken broth

Juice of 1 lemon (about 3 tablespoons)

½ teaspoon garlic powder

⅓ cup pastina or other small pasta

Fresh parsley and dill, to serve

1. Heat a large pot over medium heat. Season the chicken with ¼ teaspoon of the salt and a few turns of pepper and spray the pot with avocado oil.

2. Add the chicken to the pot, skin side down, and sear until golden brown, 5 minutes.

3. Flip the chicken and season the reverse side with ¼ teaspoon of the salt and ¼ teaspoon of the pepper. Cook for 3 more minutes.

4. While the chicken cooks, cut the carrots into ½-inch coins and roughly chop the onion and celery.

5. Remove the chicken from the pot and set on a plate. Add the carrots, onion, and celery and cook for 5 to 7 minutes, until translucent. Season with ½ teaspoon of the salt and the remaining ¼ teaspoon pepper. Stir well to get the brown bits off the bottom.

continued

6. Once the mirepoix is soft, add the garlic to the pot. Cook until fragrant, about 1 minute.

7. Pour the broth into the pot over the veggies and return the chicken to the pot. Add more broth if needed so everything is covered. Cover the pot and bring the soup to a simmer.

8. Lower the heat to a simmer and cook until the flavors combine, 30 to 35 minutes.

9. Remove the chicken from the pot and shred it with two forks. Squeeze half the lemon juice over the chicken, then season with a few turns of pepper, the remaining ¼ teaspoon salt, and the garlic powder.

10. Return the shredded chicken to the pot and add the pastina. Squeeze the remaining lemon juice into the soup and adjust the seasonings to taste. Cook until the pasta is tender, a few minutes more, then garnish with herbs to serve. Store any leftovers in an airtight container in the fridge for up to 4 days, or in the freezer for up to 3 months.

Meatball Noodle Soup

DAIRY-FREE

45 minutes | Serves 6 to 8

Little meatballs take much longer to make than you'd imagine, so if you want to make your meatballs bigger than what you see here, I'm here for it. You probably should. But if you're like me and love to futz around in the kitchen and make things that take longer than they need to because you love the process just as much as the output, make tiny meatballs like these. They fit much better on your spoon.

For the meatballs

1 pound ground beef (85/15)
1 egg
¼ red onion, very finely chopped
1 teaspoon fine sea salt
1 tablespoon Dijon mustard
1 teaspoon garlic powder
1 teaspoon paprika
½ teaspoon black pepper
2 tablespoons extra virgin olive oil
⅓ cup breadcrumbs
¼ cup oat milk
3 garlic cloves, grated
1 tablespoon lemon juice
2 tablespoons chopped parsley
2 tablespoons chopped cilantro

For the soup

1 tablespoon extra virgin olive oil
1 yellow onion, chopped
2 large carrots, chopped
½ teaspoon fine sea salt
¼ teaspoon black pepper
11 cups bone broth
1 pound medium shell pasta
Cilantro, to serve
Juice of ½ lemon, to serve (about 1½ tablespoons)

1. Make the meatballs: In a large mixing bowl, break up the beef with your fingers, being careful not to overwork it. Add the egg, onion, salt, mustard, garlic powder, paprika, pepper, olive oil, breadcrumbs, oat milk, garlic, lemon juice, parsley, and cilantro and use your hands to combine.

2. Using your fingers, roll the mixture into 1- to 2-teaspoon balls.

3. Make the soup: Heat the olive oil in a large stockpot over medium-high heat. Once the oil shimmers, add the onion and cook, until translucent, 5 to 7 minutes.

4. Add the carrots to the pot and cook until mostly softened, 5 to 7 minutes more. Season with the salt and pepper.

5. Pour the bone broth into the pot and bring to a simmer. Add the meatballs to the pot and cook until the internal temperature reaches 165°F, 15 to 20 minutes.

6. Add the pasta to the soup and cook until the pasta is tender, 10 minutes more.

7. Taste and adjust seasonings. Garnish with cilantro and lemon juice and serve immediately. Store leftovers in an airtight container in the fridge for up to 4 days, or freeze for up to 3 months.

Lasagna Soup

DAIRY-FREE

45 minutes | Serves 4 to 6

A few years ago, lasagna soup was a big trend on social media, and I just had to try making it. Since we typically don't eat meat and dairy together in our house, I adjusted it a bit to make the recipe my own. This is one of those few Italian dishes—like the Tortellini Soup (page 112)—that I prefer eating as a soup. I get the same rich, indulgent flavor profile that I crave without needing a nap afterward. It's the best of both worlds.

2 celery stalks, trimmed

2 carrots, trimmed and peeled

2 onions, trimmed

7 garlic cloves

2 tablespoons extra virgin olive oil

1 pound ground beef (85/15)

1 teaspoon fine sea salt

2 tablespoons tomato paste

2 teaspoons garlic powder

One 28-ounce can
chopped tomatoes

7 cups vegetable broth

10 dry lasagna noodles

1. Add the celery, carrots, onions, and garlic to a food processor to make the mirepoix. Pulse until the mixture is very finely chopped, like confetti.

2. In a large stockpot, heat the olive oil over medium heat. Add the ground beef and stir occasionally, until brown, about 10 minutes. Season with ½ teaspoon of the salt.

3. Once the meat has browned, remove it to a plate and add the mirepoix to the pot. Season with the remaining ½ teaspoon salt.

4. Add the tomato paste and garlic powder and cook until it deepens in color, about 1 minute.

5. Stir in the chopped tomatoes and fill the can with vegetable broth twice. Pour the vegetable broth into the pot.

6. Return the ground beef to the pot, cover the pot, and bring the soup to a boil. Reduce the heat to keep it at a simmer and cook for 30 minutes.

7. Break the lasagna noodles into small pieces and add to the pot. Cook for 8 to 10 minutes, until the noodles are al dente. Serve immediately. Store any leftovers in an airtight container in the fridge for up to 3 days or freeze for up to 3 months.

Melted Beef Soup

GLUTEN-FREE

3 hours 45 minutes | Serves 2 to 4

Adi loves slow-cooked beef like what he grew up eating. And luckily for him, the process of making it is right up my alley. When I have time, there's nothing I want to do more than tackle a recipe that feels like a big project. It's my love language—I hope you love it as much as we do.

2 pounds boneless chuck short ribs, cut into 1-inch cubes

1 teaspoon fine sea salt, plus more to taste

Black pepper

2 tablespoons avocado oil

5 leeks, dark green leaves cut off

4 carrots, cut into coins

4 celery stalks, chopped

¾ cup dry white wine

6 garlic cloves, grated with a Microplane

4 cups bone broth

1 teaspoon sweet paprika

1. Season the short ribs on all sides using ½ teaspoon of the salt and a few turns of pepper. Heat the avocado oil in a large pot over medium heat. Once the oil shimmers, add the beef and sear for 1 to 2 minutes on each side. Once seared, transfer to a plate.

2. Slice the leeks in half lengthwise and remove any layers that fall off easily (save them for later!). Add the leeks to the beef fat, cut side down, pressing to form a sear if needed. Cook until caramelized, 2 to 3 minutes per side. Remove from the pot.

3. Chop the excess leek layers and add them to the pot with the carrots and celery.

4. Season with the remaining ½ teaspoon salt and a few turns of pepper and stir to mix in the brown bits off the bottom of the pan. Cook for 5 more minutes.

5. Deglaze the pan with white wine, which should help to loosen any remaining brown bits off the bottom. Preheat the oven to 250°F.

6. Add the garlic to the pot and stir in the broth and paprika. Adjust the seasonings to taste. Return the beef and leeks to the pot. The beef should be fully submerged in liquid; if it's not, add more broth or water.

7. Bring the liquid to a simmer, then cover the pot.

8. Transfer the pot to the oven and cook for 3 hours, until the beef is fall-apart tender. Serve warm. Store any leftovers in an airtight container in the fridge for up to 4 days, or in the freezer for up to 3 months.

Taco Chili

GLUTEN-FREE

45 minutes | Serves 6

I have a confession—I don't like traditional chili. There's too much going on, and the flavor profile just isn't for me. That said, I love the *idea* of chili: the base of ground beef, beans, and veggies. I also love the process of making chili. During colder months, there's no better activity in the kitchen or meal to warm you from the inside out. It took me years to get here, but I finally have a chili recipe that I crave on the coldest days of the year, and that Adi loves just as much as I do. There's a lot about this recipe that isn't traditional—from the taco seasoning to pulsing the veggies in a food processor—but that makes me love it even more.

Taco seasoning is the only spice blend in my kitchen I regularly use. I love it. It neatly combines chili powder, cumin, paprika, garlic powder, onion powder, and oregano in one easy packet, delivering a taco experience without putting together the whole shebang. I make this all the time, and the shortcuts (food processing, taco seasoning) make it easy to whip up on a weeknight. This recipe really hits, and although it might be controversial, it's my favorite recipe in the soup section of this book. Make it for dinner tonight.

3 celery stalks, roughly chopped

2 large carrots, roughly chopped

2 small yellow onions, peeled and quartered

6 garlic cloves, peeled

1 pound ground beef (85/15)

¾ teaspoon fine sea salt, plus more to taste

Black pepper

One 15-ounce can kidney beans

One 15-ounce can cannellini beans

One 28-ounce can crushed tomatoes

1 cup bone broth

2 packets (4 tablespoons) taco seasoning

Sour cream

Sharp cheddar cheese, grated

1. Add the celery, carrots, onions, and garlic to a food processor. Pulse to finely chop. (You can also chop them finely by hand.)

2. Heat a Dutch oven over medium heat. Add the ground beef and season with ½ teaspoon of the salt and a few turns of pepper. Cook until mostly browned, breaking it up with a spoon as it cooks, 10 minutes. While the beef cooks, drain and rinse the beans.

3. Add the pulsed vegetables to the pot and season with the remaining ¼ teaspoon salt and a few more turns of pepper. Stir to combine and cook until the vegetables are soft and translucent, 5 to 7 minutes.

4. Stir in the beans and crushed tomatoes.

continued

5. Fill the empty tomato can halfway with water and add it to the pot. Pour in the bone broth as well.

6. Mix in the taco seasoning, stirring to combine. Reduce the heat to medium-low, cover the pot and let the soup simmer for 20 minutes to meld the flavors.

7. Remove the lid and raise the heat to bring the chili to a low boil. Let cook, uncovered, to reduce to your desired consistency. For a thinner chili, simmer for less time; for a thicker texture, let it reduce further.

8. Taste and adjust the seasoning, adding more salt if necessary, depending on the saltiness of your taco seasoning.

9. Serve with sour cream and shredded cheese. Store any leftovers (without garnishes) in an airtight container in the fridge for up to 3 days or freeze for up to 3 months.

 Tip   Because the level of salt in taco seasoning varies by brand, make sure to taste and adjust the seasonings as needed.

what's for dinner?

Deciding what to make for dinner is one of the most challenging parts of being a mom. And if it's a challenge for me, someone who loves to cook and thinks about food all the time, I know I'm not the only one. Adi and I feel a huge sense of responsibility to nourish our family and teach our kids about food. After all, our health is a direct result of what we put into and onto our bodies.

The recipes you'll find here are the ones I make on repeat.

Some we make more during different parts of the year, like the Low & Slow Short Ribs (page 183) in colder months; others are year-round go-tos when Adi and I are super busy rushing home from the office, like Spatchcock Chicken (page 169). I know cutting the backbone out might seem complicated, but try it once and you'll see how easy it can make your weeknight.

As a mom of younger kids and who works full time, I feel an obligation to tell you that I don't expect that you'll be able to prepare dinner from scratch seven nights a week. I know I can't. At least once a week, on days when Adi and I are both working and the kids have school, followed by activities and homework, we order in. Other nights, I cook something on the quicker side, like eggs or tortilla pizza (flour tortilla plus sauce and cheese made in the toaster or air fryer). Those recipes are not in the book for obvious reasons, but because we live in a society that makes it too easy to feel like you aren't doing enough, at the very least, I wanted you to know.

Stewed Chickpeas over Rice

VEGAN, GLUTEN-FREE

45 minutes | Serves 4

The least challenging chapter of my life as a parent was when we had a nanny. Dolma worked for us for two years, and would come and help tidy up our apartment and then pick our kids up at school and take them to the park or to their after-school activity. It was like having a third parent, and I felt like she took care of me, too. Every once in a while, she'd make us dinner. She was Tibetan and grew up in India, and loved to tell us stories about her childhood. One time, she told me that Indian women get married based on how well they roll out roti. Then she looked at my roti and told me I wouldn't be married there.

   This dish is dedicated to Dolma. I'll never forget the first time she made it for us. Adi loved it before he even tasted it, and it instantly made its way into our rotation. This is a great weeknight dinner when you're short on time—and it's cheaper and easier to get on the table than delivery.

2 tablespoons avocado oil

½ large yellow onion

2 Roma tomatoes or a handful of cherry tomatoes (about 8)

1 teaspoon fine sea salt, plus more to taste

Black pepper

Two 15.5-ounce cans chickpeas

2½ cups vegetable broth

½ teaspoon paprika

½ teaspoon cumin

½ teaspoon ground turmeric

1 teaspoon chopped fresh cilantro

White rice, to serve

1. Heat the oil in a large, high-walled pan over medium heat. Chop the onion and add it to the pan. Cook until slightly translucent, 5 to 7 minutes.

2. Add the tomatoes to the pan and season with a pinch of salt and a few turns of pepper.

3. Drain and rinse the chickpeas and add them to the pan.

4. Pour the broth over the chickpeas, give the mixture a stir, and cover the pan.

5. Cook over low heat until the tomatoes have cooked down and the chickpeas are tender, 30 minutes. (If you're busy doing other things, you can keep it cooking for up to 1 hour.)

6. Uncover the pan, stir in the paprika, cumin, turmeric, salt, and a few more turns of pepper, and cover again. Remove the pan from heat until you're ready to serve.

7. Garnish with the fresh cilantro and serve over rice. Store any leftovers in an airtight container in the fridge for up to 5 days.

Veggie Stir-Fry

VEGAN, GLUTEN-FREE

45 minutes | Serves 2 to 4

The first time I made this, I was trying to empty out our fridge. I was amazed by how good it was, and it immediately earned its spot in our rotation. Tofu lends itself so well to stir-fries, because it absorbs the flavor in the sauce and can cook as long or as little as you want. Whenever I think I have nothing to eat, I turn to this recipe. You can use any fresh, frozen, or even leftover veggies. The sauce is what makes it so delicious.

For the sauce

One 2-inch knob fresh ginger, peeled

3 garlic cloves, peeled

½ yellow onion

¼ cup tamari

¼ cup avocado oil

Juice of ½ lemon (1½ tablespoons)

3 tablespoons sesame seeds

¼ teaspoon fine sea salt, plus more to taste

For the stir-fry

One 14-ounce block extra firm tofu

1 tablespoon tamari

½ yellow onion

2 heads broccoli

2 tablespoons avocado oil

1½ cups green beans, trimmed

1 cup frozen edamame

1 cup white rice

1. Preheat to 425°F and line a baking sheet with parchment paper.

2. Make the sauce: Add the ginger, garlic, onion, tamari, avocado oil, lemon juice, sesame seeds, and salt to a blender and pulse until smooth. Taste and adjust the seasonings as needed.

3. Make the tofu: Pat the tofu dry and cut into ¾-inch cubes. Dry again and place in a bowl. Pour one-quarter of the sauce over the tofu and add the tamari. Stir to fully coat the tofu in sauce.

4. Transfer the tofu to the baking sheet and bake for 15 minutes, flipping halfway, until brown and crispy.

5. While the tofu cooks, chop the onion. Cut the broccoli, including the stems, into 1-inch pieces, and cut the green beans into 2-inch pieces.

6. Heat the avocado oil in a high-walled pan over medium heat.

7. Add the onion to the pan and cook for 5 to 7 minutes, until it starts to brown on bottom. Stir in the broccoli. Cover and cook for 3 minutes so the broccoli steams. Uncover and add the green beans, edamame, and remaining sauce, stirring to get everything coated. Cover the pan and cook over medium heat, stirring occasionally, until broccoli is tender, 10 to 15 minutes more.

8. While the veggies cook, add the rice to a small pot with 2 cups water. Bring to a simmer then cover the pot. Cook until the water is mostly absorbed and the rice is tender, 12 to 15 minutes. Remove the pot from heat and let sit, covered, for 10 minutes.

9. Remove the vegetables from the heat and add the tofu. Mix and serve over the rice. Store any leftovers in the fridge in an airtight container for up to 5 days.

Sheet Pan Salmon

GLUTEN-FREE

45 minutes | Serves 4

Sheet pan recipes don't require any time-consuming sauces or dips. Simple flavors and seasonings are all you need to highlight nature's flavors. If you're headed to the market without a dinner plan in place, just take a look at what the fish guy has and what veggies are in season, pick what looks best to you, and then turn it into a sheet pan dinner.

For the veggies

1 cup various mushrooms, cleaned and sliced

1 bunch asparagus, trimmed

3 tablespoons extra virgin olive oil

1½ teaspoons fine sea salt

3 garlic cloves, grated and divided

¾ teaspoon black pepper

1 medium zucchini, trimmed and cut into ½-inch half moons

1 cup snap peas, trimmed

For the salmon

1 pound salmon

1 teaspoon fine sea salt

½ teaspoon black pepper

Juice of 1 lemon cheek (about 2 teaspoons)

1 tablespoon avocado oil

1. Preheat the oven to 450°F, and line a baking sheet with parchment paper.

2. Add the mushrooms to one corner of the baking sheet. Place the asparagus in a large bowl and toss with 1 tablespoon of the olive oil, ½ teaspoon of the salt, 1 of the grated garlic cloves, and ¼ teaspoon of the pepper. Once coated, add to another corner of the same baking sheet.

3. Add the zucchini to the same bowl and repeat: Toss with 1 tablespoon of the olive oil, ½ teaspoon of the salt, 1 of the grated garlic cloves, and ¼ teaspoon pepper. Add to another corner of the baking sheet.

4. Repeat with the snap peas, coating them in the remaining 1 tablespoon olive oil, ½ teaspoon salt, 1 grated garlic clove, and ¼ teaspoon pepper, then add them to the last corner of the baking sheet.

5. Roast for 20 minutes, until the veggies are tender and start to brown on top.

6. Meanwhile, prepare the fish: Check the fish for bones and pat dry with a paper towel.

7. Season the fillets with the salt, pepper, and lemon juice on both sides and drizzle with the avocado oil.

8. Transfer the fish, skin side down, to the baking sheet and return to the oven. Bake for 15 minutes, until the fish flakes easily.

9. Just before serving, pop the sheet pan under the broiler on high for 3 to 5 minutes, or until everything is lightly charred on top. Serve immediately.

Chicken Fajita Lettuce Wraps

GLUTEN-FREE

1 hour | Serves 4 to 6

I love any excuse to fill a salad cup like a taco and add a dollop of sour cream or avocado. And as the one on dishwasher duty seven days a week, I also love a meal that comes together in one pan. You can let it simmer if you have the time, or throw it all together and have it ready in under an hour. It's delicious, nutritious, and everyone in the family will love it. Just kidding. My kids won't eat this, but maybe yours will.

2 tablespoons extra virgin olive oil

1 medium yellow onion, finely chopped

1 red bell pepper, finely chopped

8 garlic cloves, minced

2 pounds boneless, skinless chicken breasts or ground chicken

Juice of 1 lemon cheek (about 2 teaspoons)

2 tablespoons taco seasoning

2 cups vegetable or chicken broth

⅓ cup white rice

1 ripe avocado, to serve

2 to 3 heads baby butter lettuce

Sour cream, to serve

Chives, to serve

1. Heat the olive oil in a large pan over medium heat and add the onion and bell pepper. Cook, stirring occasionally, until they begin to soften, 5 to 7 minutes.

2. Add the garlic to the pan and cook until fragrant, 1 to 2 minutes.

3. While the veggies cook, finely chop the chicken so it's almost the texture of ground chicken.

4. Squeeze a lemon cheek over the chicken and add it to the pan. Stir in the taco seasoning.

5. Add the broth and rice to the pan and increase the heat to medium-high. Stir everything together so it's well combined.

6. Bring the mixture to a boil, then lower the heat and cover. Cook until the sauce has thickened and the rice is fully cooked, 20 to 30 minutes. Keep warm until you're ready to serve.

7. Slice the avocado and spoon the fajita mixture into the butter lettuce leaves. Garnish with sour cream, chives, and the avocado.

Moo Shu–ish Chicken & Rice

GLUTEN-FREE*

45 minutes | Serves 4

I spend a lot of time trying to figure out what to feed my family for dinner. One day, while I was brainstorming at work, I dreamed up this moo shu–inspired chicken. I thought I had ground chicken in the fridge, but when I got home, I realized I only had chicken breasts, so I improvised and cut them into small pieces—it turned into an even better dinner than I imagined. The finely chopped chicken was much juicier and absorbed so much flavor. Even though cutting it into small pieces is an extra step, it's totally worth it. You can eat it in a lettuce cup instead or over rice, as I have it here. Then take the leftovers to work the next day!

2 pounds boneless, skinless chicken breasts

1 bunch scallions, trimmed

1 red bell pepper

11 baby bok choy

2 tablespoons extra virgin olive oil

½ teaspoon fine sea salt

¼ teaspoon black pepper

¾ tablespoon cornstarch

1 cup basmati rice

For the marinade

1 teaspoon garlic powder

1 teaspoon minced ginger

4 garlic cloves, grated

Juice of ½ lemon (about 1½ tablespoons)

3 tablespoons tamari

3 tablespoons hoisin sauce

½ teaspoon fine sea salt

¼ teaspoon black pepper

1. Cut the chicken into ½-inch cubes and place in a large bowl.

2. Make the marinade: Whisk together the garlic powder, ginger, garlic, lemon juice, tamari, hoison, salt, and pepper in a small bowl and pour over the chicken. Stir to coat the chicken. Let sit for 10 to 15 minutes while the chicken comes to room temperature.

3. Meanwhile, prep your veggies. Cut the scallions into ¼-inch pieces, and finely chop the bell pepper and bok choy.

4. Heat the olive oil in a large frying pan over medium heat.

5. Add the bell pepper, bok choy, and scallions to the pan and cook until slightly wilted, about 3 to 5 minutes. Season with the salt and pepper.

 Note To make this gluten-free, make sure to use GF-certified hoisin sauce.

continued

6. Add the marinated chicken to the pan and cook for over medium heat, until slightly golden on the outside and fully cooked, 7 to 8 minutes.

7. Whisk the cornstarch together with ¾ tablespoon water to make a slurry. This will thicken the sauce. Stir into the pan and cook for a few minutes, until the sauce thickens to your liking. Taste and adjust seasonings.

8. Place the rice in a fine-mesh strainer and rinse until the water runs clear. Transfer to a pot with 1½ cups water. Place over medium-high heat and bring to a boil.

9. Lower the heat to a simmer, cover the pot and cook until the water is absorbed, 12 minutes. Remove from the heat but keep the lid on to allow the rice to steam for 10 minutes. Fluff the rice with a fork.

10. Spoon the chicken over the rice and serve immediately. Store any leftovers in an airtight container in the fridge for up to 5 days.

Chicken Schnitzel

1 hour | Serves 4

If Adi's making dinner, it's probably steak or schnitzel. It's one of our favorite meals in the rotation. My daughter only likes it when he makes it, and honestly, I'm fine with that. Sometimes I even plant the idea in her head so that she'll request it and I won't have to cook!

Schnitzel is one of those dishes that shows up in many cultures. Fundamentally, it's thinly pounded meat, breaded and pan-fried. In New Jersey, it's called a chicken cutlet. It's incredibly common in Israel, so Adi grew up with it. His mom always wants to make it for our kids—it was such a thrill when they finally started eating it.

Adi seasons the flour, egg, and breadcrumbs individually, so every layer of the schnitzel has flavor. Using the bag to pound the chicken is my trick—I find it easier and cleaner. He pounds it on a cutting board with a layer of parchment over it. Do whatever works best for you! We usually serve it with pasta (and of course, Rao's) and steamed broccoli. I dip mine in ketchup. It's so good.

4 boneless, skinless chicken breasts (about 2 pounds)

3 large eggs

2 teaspoons fine sea salt

1 teaspoon Dijon mustard

Splash of tamari

1 teaspoon sweet paprika

1 teaspoon lemon juice, plus more to serve

1 cup all-purpose flour

2 cups unseasoned breadcrumbs

1½ cups avocado or canola oil, for frying

Steamed broccoli, to serve

1. Place a chicken breast in a large resealable bag and use a meat mallet to pound it into an even ¼-inch layer. Repeat with the remaining breasts.

2. Set up your dredging station. Crack 3 eggs into a bowl and season with ¼ teaspoon of the salt, the Dijon mustard, tamari, paprika, and lemon juice. Whisk it all together with a fork.

3. Add the flour to a large dinner plate and season with ½ teaspoon of the salt. Stir it together with a fork.

4. Add the breadcrumbs to another dinner plate and season with ½ teaspoon of the salt.

continued

5. You'll dredge the chicken in the following order: flour, egg, breadcrumbs. As you do it, try to keep one hand reserved for dry ingredients and the other for wet. Otherwise, it can get messy!

6. Take the first chicken cutlet and coat it in flour. Make sure to get it fully covered. Shake off any excess.

7. Transfer the chicken to the egg mixture and cover entirely in egg, flipping to coat both sides. No dry spots should remain.

8. Carefully move the chicken to the plate with breadcrumbs and press the crumbs into the chicken. You'll want to use a little force here so the breadcrumbs stick. Place the coated chicken on a plate or baking sheet lined with parchment paper while you bread the rest of the chicken.

9. Repeat the process with the remaining cutlets.

10. Pour avocado oil into a medium or large frying pan so you have a ½-inch layer (the exact amount of oil you need depends on the size of your pan). While the oil heats, set up a baking sheet with a wire rack over it. Heat the oil to 350°F (the oil should be shimmering), then add the first cutlet to the pan. Cook until golden brown 2 to 3 minutes. Flip and repeat on the other side, cooking for 2 to 3 minutes more.

11. Transfer the schnitzel to the wire rack with tongs and season with the remaining salt.

12. Repeat this process three more times, until all the schnitzel is cooked. Serve with steamed broccoli and a squeeze of lemon juice. Store any leftovers in the fridge in an airtight container for up to 3 days; reheat in the oven at 375°F for 10 to 15 minutes or in the air fryer at 350°F for 4 to 6 minutes.

 Tip Adi adds a 2-inch piece of raw carrot to the frying pan just before adding the schnitzel to prevent the oil from burning. It really works!

Sheet Pan Chicken

GLUTEN-FREE

1 hour 30 minutes | Serves 4

At least once a week, I'll stare into my fridge, look to see what proteins and veggies I have, and throw them all on a sheet pan. It's a fast, easy way to serve a nutritious and delicious dinner to my family.

The most important thing to master when you're making a sheet pan dinner is the cook times. Potatoes take much longer to cook than asparagus or string beans. I like to keep the veggies divided into their own sections on the pan so I can add them at the right time. That way, everything cooks perfectly.

I use a lot of the same spices and seasonings in my recipes (sweet paprika, garlic powder, and oregano are my tried-and-true favorites). If there's something in this recipe you don't like, feel free to change it up. It's the method that's most important here. Whenever I make this, I think of the sheet pan cornflake chicken my grandmother used to make for me when I was little; it was one of her go-to chicken dishes. This is mine.

For the potatoes

1½ pounds Yukon gold potatoes (about 6)
3 garlic cloves, grated
1 tablespoon avocado oil
½ teaspoon fine sea salt
¼ teaspoon black pepper

For the chicken & veggies

Juice of 1 lemon (about 3 tablespoons)
2 tablespoons avocado oil
1 tablespoon Dijon mustard
4 garlic cloves, grated
¾ teaspoon fine sea salt, plus more to taste
¼ teaspoon black pepper, plus more to taste

1 teaspoon garlic powder
½ teaspoon ground turmeric
1 teaspoon sweet paprika
1 teaspoon dried oregano
1½ pounds bone-in, skin-on whole chicken legs (about 2)
1 bunch broccolini, or 1 head broccoli
12 ounces green beans

continued

1. Preheat the oven to 425°F. Line a baking sheet with parchment paper.

2. Make the potatoes: Wash the potatoes well and cut into 2-inch cubes. Add the potatoes to a large bowl and add the grated garlic, oil, salt, and pepper.

3. Mix well with your hands so the potatoes are fully coated, then transfer to the prepared baking sheet.

4. Roast the potatoes for 30 minutes.

5. While the potatoes cook, prepare the chicken: Combine the lemon juice, oil, mustard, garlic, ½ teaspoon of the salt, the pepper, garlic powder, turmeric, paprika, and oregano in a large bowl and whisk until smooth.

6. Pat the chicken dry with paper towels and add to the bowl. Coat the chicken well with the spice mixture.

7. Place the chicken on the pan with the potatoes, with the skin side up so it gets crispy.

8. Return the pan to the oven and bake for 10 minutes.

9. Meanwhile, trim the broccolini and green beans, then add them to the leftover chicken marinade.

10. Season with the remaining ¼ teaspoon salt and a few turns of pepper and stir to coat them in the sauce.

11. After 10 minutes, remove the pan from the oven and add the veggies. Return it to the oven and cook for another 25 to 30 minutes, until the internal temperature of the chicken reaches 165°F.

12. Turn the oven to the broil setting. Transfer the potatoes and veggies to a serving plate. Broil the chicken on high just until crispy, 3 to 5 minutes.

13. Add the crispy chicken to the plate with the veggies and serve. Store any leftovers in an airtight container in the fridge for 3 to 5 days.

One-Pot Spring Chicken

GLUTEN-FREE

2 hours 25 minutes | Serves 4 to 6

I love a one-pot chicken dish. It's one of my favorite ways to throw together a meal for my family when I'm working from home. This one in particular is one of my favorites, because it incorporates fresh veggies from the farmers market.

The most important part of successfully executing this dish is adding the veggies at the right time. You want them to be cooked, but you don't want them to lose their vibrant green color, and you want them to be crunchy. That's why I add them at the very end, when the chicken is finished cooking. It comes out perfect every time.

4 whole chicken legs, skin-on

1½ teaspoons fine sea salt

½ teaspoon black pepper, plus more to season

1 yellow onion, chopped

3 garlic cloves, chopped

½ cup white wine

2 cups basmati rice

¼ teaspoon sweet paprika

2 cups bone broth

2 ears of corn, cut off the cob

1 cup sugar snap peas, cut on the bias

1 medium zucchini, cut into cubes

1 cup peas, either from shelling peas or frozen, thawed

2 tablespoons extra virgin olive oil

1 teaspoon dried oregano

1 teaspoon garlic powder

Juice of 1 lemon cheek (about 2 teaspoons)

1. Preheat the oven to 300°F.

2. Pat the chicken legs dry with paper towels. Season all sides using ½ teaspoon of the salt and a few turns of pepper.

3. Heat a large braiser over medium-high heat and add the chicken, skin-side down. Cook until golden brown, 8 minutes. Flip the chicken and sear the other side.

4. Once seared, remove the chicken from the pan and add the onion. Lower the heat to medium and cook until translucent, 5 to 7 minutes. Add the garlic and cook until aromatic, 1 minute.

5. Pour in the white wine and stir to get the brown bits off the bottom of the pan. Cook until the wine has mostly reduced, about 5 minutes.

6. Stir in the rice. Season with ½ teaspoon of the salt, ¼ teaspoon of the pepper, and the paprika. Toast for 1 to 2 minutes, until fragrant.

continued

7. Add the chicken back to the pan, skin-side up, and push it in so the meat touches the bottom of the pan.

8. Pour in the broth and stir to combine. Cover the pan and bake for 2 hours.

9. While the chicken cooks, add the corn, snap peas, zucchini, and green peas to a large bowl with the olive oil, the remaining ½ teaspoon of salt, ¼ teaspoon of the pepper, the oregano, garlic powder, and lemon juice. Stir to combine.

10. After 1 hour, remove the chicken from the oven. Turn the oven to the broil setting. Add the veggies to the top, stirring them into the rice slightly. Make sure the chicken skin is exposed and broil on low for 10 minutes, until the veggies are slightly soft and chicken skin is crispy. Serve immediately. Store any leftovers in an airtight container in the fridge for up to 3 days.

How to Spatchcock a Chicken

I know spatchcocking sounds complicated, but once you get comfortable with the idea of cutting the backbone out of a bird, you, too, will make this dish all the time. A good pair of sharp kitchen shears is nonnegotiable. Follow the guide below to know exactly where to cut, and you can even save the backbone for stock.

Once the bone is cut out, flip the bird, pull the breasts toward you, and press it down flat until you hear a crack. The bird will stay flat and cook evenly in a fraction of the time.

Cut along these lines to remove the backbone.

Spatchcock Chicken

GLUTEN-FREE

1 hour | Serves 6

A spatchcock chicken is a once-a-week meal in the Ben-Ishay house, especially in the winter when I want a cozy, home-cooked dinner that tastes like it took a lot of effort. The way I see it, it's really just two ingredients—chicken and potatoes—with your favorite seasonings. This recipe has become my go-to dinner for those crazy days when I feel like I have no time to get a hearty meal on the table for my family. Everybody loves it. My kids love the chicken, and Adi especially loves the melt-in-your-mouth potatoes. Creamy Yukon gold potatoes cooked in roasted chicken juices are the ultimate comfort food in our house, and once my kids dare try them, they won't believe they missed out on them for so long. Did I mention it takes just about an hour, start to finish? And most of that time is spent waiting for the chicken to come out of the oven.

4- to 5-pound whole chicken, giblets removed

Juice of 2 lemons (about ⅓ cup)

¼ cup avocado oil

2 tablespoons Dijon mustard

8 garlic cloves, grated

1½ teaspoons fine sea salt, plus more to taste

½ teaspoon black pepper, plus more to taste

2 teaspoons garlic powder

1 teaspoon ground turmeric

2 teaspoons sweet paprika

2 teaspoons dried oregano

3 large Yukon gold potatoes

1. Preheat the oven to 425°F, and line a baking sheet with parchment paper.

2. Using sharp kitchen shears, cut the backbone out of the chicken. Flatten it on a cutting board and push the breastbone down until you hear it crack. The chicken should stay flat.

3. Combine the lemon juice, oil, mustard, garlic, salt, pepper, garlic powder, turmeric, paprika, and oregano in a large bowl and whisk until smooth.

4. Pat the chicken dry with paper towels and coat the chicken well with the spice mixture. Use your hands to get it completely covered.

5. Place the chicken on the prepared pan with the skin side up.

continued

6. Cut the potatoes into ⅓-inch rounds and add them to the bowl with the leftover marinade. Drizzle a little olive oil over the potatoes and season with ½ teaspoon salt and a few turns of pepper. Use your hands to coat the potatoes in the remaining marinade.

7. Surround the chicken with the sliced potatoes and bake for 45 minutes to 1 hour, until the internal temperature of the chicken breast reaches 165°F.

8. Remove the chicken from the pan and flip the potatoes. Return the potatoes to the oven and cook for 10 to 15 minutes, until golden brown. Rest the chicken while the potatoes cook.

9. When the potatoes are finished, transfer them to plates and slice the chicken to serve. Save the remaining meat for the chicken salad and soup, and save the bones for Chicken Broth (page 101). They'll keep in the fridge in an airtight container for up to 5 days.

One-Pot Golden Chicken & Rice

GLUTEN-FREE

2 hours 25 minutes | Serves 4 to 6

One-pot chicken dinners like this and the One-Pot Spring Chicken (page 165) are on repeat in my house. They're the perfect set-it-and-forget-it meals. This one is packed with ginger, turmeric, and coconut, inspired by one of my favorite chicken soup recipes (page 123).

I always make it in my Staub braiser, which makes searing the chicken and veggies much more fun. I love the sizzle! That pan lives on my stove—we use it all the time. This is such a great dinner to make when you're working from home: sear everything when you have a quick break or while you're on a call, pop it in the oven, then when your family comes home, dinner's ready.

1 tablespoon extra virgin olive oil

4 bone-in, skin-on chicken thighs

1 teaspoon fine sea salt

½ teaspoon black pepper

1 yellow onion

2 large carrots

2 celery stalks

1 teaspoon cumin

3 teaspoon ground turmeric

1 teaspoon garlic powder

7 to 10 garlic cloves, grated

One 1-inch knob fresh ginger, grated

1 cup basmati rice

2 cups vegetable broth

½ cup full-fat coconut milk

Juice of 1 lemon (about 3 tablespoons)

Chopped cilantro, to serve

2 lemon slices, to serve

1. Preheat the oven to 300°F.

2. Pat the chicken dry with paper towels. Season all sides using ½ teaspoon of salt and a few turns of pepper, about ¼ teaspoon.

3. Heat the olive oil in a large braiser over medium-high heat and add the chicken, skin-side down. Cook for 8 minutes, until golden brown. Flip the chicken and sear the other side. Remove the chicken from the pan and set on a plate.

4. Chop the onion, carrots, and celery and add them to the same pan. Cook over medium heat until the onions are translucent, about 5 to 7 minutes. Season with ½ teaspoon salt and a few turns of pepper, about ¼ teaspoon.

5. Stir in the cumin, turmeric, and garlic powder, and cook for about a minute until fragrant. Add the grated garlic and ginger and mix well.

6. Stir in the rice and cook for 1 to 2 minutes to toast, then add the broth, coconut milk, and lemon juice.

7. Return the chicken to the pan skin side up, making sure it's submerged in liquid as far as it can go.

8. Cover the pan and transfer to the oven. Cook for 1 hour. When it's finished, the rice will be tender and the liquid fully absorbed.

9. Top with chopped cilantro and a squeeze of lemon juice right before serving.

Pesto Chicken Meatballs

DAIRY-FREE

1 hour | Serves 4

Ramps have a very short season in early spring. I started using them more in my cooking when I did a demo at Bethel Woods in the Catskills (where Woodstock took place!). The wild onion grows like crazy up there, and these meatballs are an incredible way to use them. I added ramps to the meatballs and the pesto, so it adds as much flavor to these meatballs as possible. If you want to make this when they aren't in season, replace with basil or scallions (or a combination).

For the purée & pesto

2 bunches ramps, roughly chopped (about 1 cup)

3 garlic cloves

1 teaspoon fine sea salt

¼ teaspoon black pepper

¼ cup extra virgin olive oil

Juice of 1 lemon (about 3 tablespoons)

¼ cup pine nuts

¼ cup nutritional yeast

1 cup fresh spinach

For the meatballs

1 pound organic ground chicken

1 egg

½ cup breadcrumbs

Olive oil spray

1 cup orzo

1. Make the purée: Add the ramps, garlic, ½ teaspoon of the salt, the pepper, olive oil, and lemon juice to a food processor and pulse until smooth. Reserve ½ cup for the meatballs.

2. Make the pesto: With the remaining purée in the food processor, add the pine nuts, nutritional yeast, remaining ½ teaspoon salt, and spinach and pulse to combine.

3. Preheat the air fryer to 420°F or the oven to 450°F. Line a sheet pan with parchment paper.

4. In a large bowl, combine the chicken, egg, ½ cup reserved ramp purée, and the breadcrumbs. Mix together with your hands and let it come to room temperature.

5. Roll the meatballs into 1-inch balls and place on the parchment paper–lined tray.

6. Spray the meatballs with olive oil spray.

7. Air-fry for 16 minutes, until the meatballs are golden and the internal temperature reaches 165°F. In the oven, bake for 20 to 22 minutes, flipping halfway.

8. While the meatballs cook, bring a pot of water to a boil and add the orzo. Cook for 8 to 10 minutes, until al dente.

9. Add the pesto to a large bowl. Remove the meatballs from the air fryer or oven and immediately toss them in the bowl with the pesto.

10. Serve the meatballs with orzo. Store any leftovers in an airtight container in the fridge for up to 3 days.

Steak Tacos & Adi's Crazy Hot Sauce

25 minutes | Serves 2 to 4

Taco night at our house is a great excuse to give everyone exactly what they want for dinner. You can just slice up the protein, heat up tortillas, and whip up a quick slaw, then let everyone create their own meal.

Our kids are spoiled rotten and love rib eye and filet mignon. I love to serve these tacos with Taco Slaw (page 32), but use whatever veggies you have in the fridge.

Adi's letting me share his hot sauce recipe here, too. If you like spicy (he does, I don't), you'll love it. He uses whatever peppers look best (and hottest) at the store, and in the summer, you can find them at the farmers market. Control the heat based on what you like: Jalapeños and serranos are a bit more mild; habaneros and scotch bonnets bring more heat.

1 pound rib eye, about 1½ to 2 inches thick

½ teaspoon fine sea salt

¼ teaspoon black pepper

1 tablespoon avocado oil or another neutral oil

Taco Slaw, page 32

Flour tortillas, to serve

1 ripe avocado, sliced

For Adi's crazy hot sauce

10 to 12 small peppers (2 to 3 each of a mix of habaneros, jalapeños, serranos, etc.)

1 head garlic, peeled

1 red onion, peeled and cut in half

1 large handful parsley

1 large handful cilantro

2 tablespoons red pepper flakes

Juice of ½ lemon (about 1½ tablespoons)

1 tablespoon extra virgin olive oil

Fine sea salt and black pepper

1. Remove the rib eye from the fridge 30 to 45 minutes before you start cooking to bring it to room temperature. Preheat the oven to 275°F. Line a baking sheet with parchment paper.

2. Pat the rib eye dry with a paper towel and season on both sides with the salt and pepper.

3. Place the rib eye on the prepared baking sheet.

4. Bake for 25 to 30 minutes, until the internal temperature of the meat is 120°F for medium-rare. While the steak is in the oven, heat the avocado oil in a frying or cast iron pan over medium-high heat.

5. Remove the steak from the oven and sear in the pan for 1 minute on each side to form a nice crust. Don't touch it while it's searing, so a crust can form.

6. Take the steak off the pan and let rest for 10 minutes.

7. While the steak rests, make Adi's crazy hot sauce: Remove the stems from the peppers and place in a large blender with the garlic cloves, onion, parsley, cilantro, pepper flakes, lemon juice, and olive oil. Pulse to combine until no big chunks remain. Season with salt and pepper to taste.

8. To make the tacos, slice the rib eye and pile the steak and slaw on the tortillas. Top with the avocado slices and crazy sauce, if you dare.

Magic Meat Sauce with Rice

GLUTEN-FREE

40 minutes | Serves 2 to 4

This is the recipe that finally got my daughter to eat onions, garlic, and broth without even knowing it. Which is why I call it magic meat sauce.

   This sauce is great for kids who like meat sauce and think they don't like anything else. I decided to blend the onion and garlic because my little one doesn't like "thingies" in her food—she wants everything completely smooth. The first time you make it, follow the recipe step-by-step, but once you get the hang of it, throw in whatever veggies you have. Don't skip the sweet paprika! That's what disguises the sauce and makes it red.

1 pound ground beef (85/15)
1 teaspoon fine sea salt
1½ cups beef bone broth
1 onion, cut in half
5 garlic cloves
1 teaspoon sweet paprika
1 cup white rice

1. Heat a large frying pan over medium heat.

2. Add the beef to the pan and break it up with a wooden spoon, cooking until brown, 10 minutes. Stir in the salt.

3. Add the bone broth, onion, and garlic to a blender and pulse until smooth.

4. Once the meat has mostly browned, add the sweet paprika to the pan and cook until aromatic, about 1 minute.

5. Pour the bone broth mixture into the pan and bring to a boil. Once boiling, lower the heat and cover the pan. Simmer so all the flavors combine and the sauce thickens slightly, at least 30 minutes and up to 3 hours.

6. About 20 minutes before you're ready to serve, add the rice to a small pot with 2 cups water. Bring to a simmer, then cover the pot. Cook until the water is mostly absorbed and the rice is tender, 12 to 15 minutes. Remove the pot from heat and leave covered for 10 minutes.

7. Fluff the rice with a fork and serve with the meat sauce on top.

8. Store leftovers in an airtight container in the refrigerator for up to 3 days.

Spaghetti & Meatballs with Magic Sauce

DAIRY-FREE

1 hour | Serves 6

Spaghetti and meatballs has been in my dinner rotation my entire life. My mom made it on repeat, and now I do, too. It's a classic. When my kids were younger, I had to get creative to get more veggies on their plates. I blended up whatever I had in the fridge into a smooth, vibrant sauce that looks just as good as it tastes. It's magic because it allows you to get more veggies in, use what you have, and jam-pack your meal with nutrients. And if you don't feel like making the sauce, I won't judge you for using a jar of Rao's. That's what I'd do.

1 yellow onion, cut into large 2-inch pieces

5 garlic cloves, peeled

2 tablespoons extra virgin olive oil

1 pound ground beef (85/15)

1 pound ground lamb

1 large egg

1 teaspoon fine sea salt

1 teaspoon sweet paprika

1 teaspoon garlic powder

1 teaspoon dried oregano

¼ teaspoon black pepper

1 tablespoon Dijon mustard

⅓ cup breadcrumbs

½ teaspoon baking soda

1 pound spaghetti, to serve

1. Preheat the oven to 400°F, and line a baking sheet with parchment paper.

2. Add the onion and garlic to a food processor and pulse until finely chopped.

3. Pour in 1 tablespoon of the olive oil and pulse again.

4. Place the ground beef and lamb in a large bowl.

5. In a small bowl, whisk together the egg, salt, paprika, garlic powder, oregano, and pepper.

6. Pour the egg mixture over the ground meat and add the garlic/onion paste. Add the remaining 1 tablespoon olive oil, the mustard, breadcrumbs, and baking soda. Use your hands to combine until everything is fully incorporated.

7. Roll the mixture into 1-inch balls and place on the prepared baking sheet (it's fine for the meatballs to be close together).

8. Bake for 15 to 20 minutes, until the meatballs are seared brown on top and cooked through.

continued

For the sauce

2 tablespoons extra virgin olive oil

1 yellow onion, diced

1 carrot, cut into ½-inch coins

1 red bell pepper, diced

2 large tomatoes, chopped, or 2 pints
　　cherry tomatoes, chopped

4 garlic cloves, chopped

¼ cup tomato paste (optional)

½ to 1 teaspoon fine sea salt, or to taste

1 teaspoon garlic powder

1 tablespoon sweet paprika

2 teaspoons dried oregano

2 cups vegetable broth

9. While the meatballs cook, get the sauce ready: Heat the olive oil in a large frying pan over medium heat.

10. Add the onion, carrot, and bell pepper to the pan and cook until the onion is translucent, about 7 minutes. Stir in the tomatoes and garlic.

11. Add the tomato paste and spices and cook until the red deepens in color, about 1 minute more.

12. Stir in the broth, lower the heat slightly, and cover the pan. Cook until all the veggies are soft and cooked through, 10 minutes.

13. Carefully transfer the mixture to a blender and pulse until smooth.

14. Return the sauce to the pan and bring to a low simmer. When the meatballs are ready, add them to the sauce and keep over low heat until you're ready to serve.

15. Just before serving, bring a large pot of water to a boil and add the spaghetti. Cook for 10 to 11 minutes, until al dente.

16. Serve the meatballs and sauce over the spaghetti. Store any leftovers in an airtight container in the fridge for 3 to 5 days.

Low & Slow Short Ribs

30 minutes active, 4 hours total | Serves 4

Whenever I see short ribs on the menu or at the store, I think of Adi. He loves them. While my mom made pot roast for us growing up, Adi's mom made tender, fall-off-the-bone short ribs. When I want to do something special for him—and when I want to turn a meal into a project —I make these short ribs. They aren't super complicated, but the time and effort you put into them translates to love. Every bite tastes like a hug, which is how Adi and I show our love for each other, our friends, and our family. If you like pot roast but have never made short ribs, you're in for a treat.

2 pounds boneless chuck short ribs

1½ teaspoons fine sea salt, plus more to taste

½ teaspoon black pepper, plus more to taste

1 tablespoon avocado oil

1 yellow onion, roughly chopped

6 garlic cloves, roughly chopped

1 tablespoon tomato paste

1 tablespoon balsamic vinegar

2 tablespoons all-purpose flour

1 cup red wine

1 cup beef bone broth

1 teaspoon Herbes de Provence

1 teaspoon sweet paprika

1 teaspoon honey

2 bay leaves

3 Yukon Gold potatoes

2 carrots

1. Preheat the oven to 300°F.

2. Cut the short ribs into 1-inch cubes and season with ½ teaspoon of the salt and ¼ teaspoon of the pepper.

3. Heat the avocado oil in a Dutch oven over medium heat until shimmering. Add the meat to the pan and cook for 1 to 2 minutes on each side to sear.

4. Remove the meat from the pan with tongs, transfer to a plate, and add the onion to the pot. Cook until translucent, 5 to 7 minutes. Add the garlic and cook until aromatic, 1 minute more.

5. Stir in the tomato paste and balsamic vinegar and cook until the tomato paste deepens in color, 1 minute more.

6. Sprinkle the flour over everything and stir to combine. Cook for 1 to 2 more minutes (the flour should be completely incorporated), then pour in the wine, broth, and 1 cup water.

continued

7. Add the Herbes de Provence, the remaining 1 teaspoon salt, remaining ¼ teaspoon pepper, the sweet paprika, honey, and bay leaves, and stir.

8. Return the meat to the pot and make sure it's completely submerged in liquid. Cover the pot and place in the oven. Cook for 2½ hours.

9. When the cooking time is almost up, peel the potatoes and carrots. Cut them into 1-inch pieces.

10. Add the potatoes and carrots to the pot and make sure they're submerged in liquid. Season with a pinch of salt and pepper and cover.

11. Return the pot to the oven and cook for another hour, until the potatoes and carrots are fork-tender. Remove the bay leaves. Taste and adjust seasonings as needed, then serve immediately. Store any leftovers in an airtight container in the fridge for 3 to 5 days or freeze for up to 3 months.

Lamb Ragu

GLUTEN-FREE

30 minutes active, 5 hours total | Serves 4

Before Adi and I had kids, we could spend an entire Sunday cooking. We'd call it one-meal Sundays and would have friends over to eat. We loved being in the kitchen cooking together— it's where we fell in love. Slow-cooked lamb was often on the menu for those meals. I'd go to the Whole Foods in Chelsea and get a lamb shoulder to braise as we cooked the rest of the meal.

This recipe pays homage to those slow Sundays, but this one comes together much faster. Whenever I taste it, it still brings me back to those days (now almost twenty years ago). My youngest loves this dish, too. I'll never forget her watching me eat it when she was a toddler, telling me, "Mommy, I'll try that. Can I try?" It was the cutest thing. I'll make it for her any day.

1 tablespoon extra virgin olive oil

2 large carrots

2 medium yellow onions

3 celery stalks

1 pound lamb loin

1 teaspoon fine sea salt,
  plus more to taste

1 teaspoon black pepper

9 garlic cloves, finely chopped

1 teaspoon oregano

1 teaspoon garlic powder

1 teaspoon onion powder

1 tablespoon sweet paprika

2 tablespoons tomato paste

1 cup Pinot Noir

4 cups vegetable broth

Pasta, rice, or polenta, to serve

1. Preheat the oven to 250°F. Heat the olive oil in a large stockpot over medium heat.

2. Roughly chop the carrots, onions, and celery.

3. Once the oil shimmers, add the lamb to the pot and season all sides with the salt and ¼ teaspoon of the pepper. Cook for 2 to 3 minutes on each side to create a sear.

4. Remove the lamb from the pot, transfer to a plate, and add the carrots, onion, and celery to the stockpot.

5. Cook the vegetables until translucent, 5 to 7 minutes. Add the garlic and cook until fragrant, about 1 minute.

6. Stir in the spices and tomato paste and cook until the tomato paste caramelizes and turns a deep red color, 1 to 2 minutes more.

continued

7. Pour in the wine and cover. Cook for 2 to 3 minutes, until simmering.

8. Return the lamb to the pot and add the vegetable broth. Spoon the veggies and liquid over the lamb, then cover the pot and bring to a boil.

9. Once boiling, remove from the heat and place the covered pot in the oven. Cook for 4½ hours. The lamb is done when it falls off the bone easily.

10. Remove the lamb from the pot and transfer to a bowl or plate.

11. Set the pot over medium heat until the sauce is reduced by half, 10 to 15 minutes.

12. Carefully transfer the sauce to a blender and purée until smooth. It should be deep orange in color and look like a thin soup.

13. Pour the blended sauce back into the pot and cook for 10 to 15 minutes to further reduce the sauce until it coats the back of a spoon.

14. Shred the lamb using a fork. Either stir the lamb into the sauce or place it on top to serve. Serve over pasta, rice, or any other grain you love. Store the leftover lamb together with the sauce in an airtight container. It will save for 3 to 4 days in the fridge, or 2 months in the freezer.

Melted Beef Bolognese

DAIRY-FREE

45 minutes active, 4 hour 15 minutess total | Serves 4

This dish has the bones of beef stew, transformed into pasta. The more you cook, the more you'll realize how many similarities there are between dishes across cultures. It's part of what I love about food. The first time I made beef stew I was shocked by how delicious it was. This recipe is similar to the Low & Slow Short Ribs (page 183); by stirring in angel hair, you get an incredibly delicious, creamy sauce (with no cream, obviously). Oftentimes, when I'm making this for dinner, Adi doesn't even wait for the pasta to cook—he comes into the kitchen and immediately stuffs the meat in a pita. You could do the same.

1 pound boneless chuck short ribs

1 teaspoon fine sea salt, plus more to taste

Black pepper

1 tablespoon avocado oil

1 medium carrot, peeled

1 medium yellow onion

2 celery stalks

3 garlic cloves, grated with a Microplane

½ cup red wine

1 teaspoon balsamic vinegar

1½ cups marinara sauce

1½ cups bone broth

1 pound angel hair pasta, to serve

Parsley, to garnish, if you're feeling fancy

1. Preheat the oven to 250°F. Set a large braiser or Dutch oven on the stove over medium-high heat.

2. Pat the short ribs dry on both sides with a paper towel and season all over with ½ teaspoon of the salt and a few turns of pepper. Drizzle with the avocado oil. Set the meat in the hot braiser and sear on both sides until golden brown, 2 to 3 minutes per side. The short ribs should easily lift out of the pan. Transfer the meat to a plate.

A Note on Tomato Sauce

I most often use Rao's marinara sauce in recipes like this because that's what I have in the pantry. Use your favorite tomato sauce, or opt for canned puréed or whole tomatoes. For the latter, taste as you go and adjust the seasonings, since you won't have the same flavors as a marinara sauce.

continued

3. While the meat cooks, use the wide holes of a box grater to shred the carrot, onion, and celery.

4. After you've removed the meat, add the carrot, onion, and celery to the braiser and cook until mostly translucent, about 5 to 7 minutes. Season with the remaining ½ teaspoon salt and a few turns of pepper.

5. Stir in the garlic, wine, and balsamic vinegar and cook until the wine reduces by half, about 5 minutes.

6. Pour in the marinara sauce and broth, then return the meat to the pot. Make sure the meat is mostly covered by the sauce. Bring the sauce to a boil.

7. Cover the pot and transfer to the oven. Cook for 3½ hours, until the meat falls apart easily. Taste and adjust the seasonings as needed.

8. To serve, remove the meat from the pot and shred using two forks. Return the braiser to the stove and add the angel hair directly to the sauce. Cook for 2 to 4 minutes, until the pasta is al dente. Transfer the pasta to a plate and top with the shredded beef, then spoon the sauce over. Garnish with parsley (if desired, just for color!). Store any leftovers in an airtight container in the fridge for 3 to 5 days or freeze for up to 3 months.

how to eat leftovers

According to my mom, I've always loved leftovers. She often tells a story about when I was really little and she would slice up leftover meatballs to make a sandwich. We'd sit at the kitchen table and eat lunch together, and I would lick my lips because it was so good.

What I remember is complaining about leftovers when I was older. I felt robbed of a new, delicious meal. But I was so wrong—leftovers are the most underrated ingredient in your fridge. When you use leftovers as an ingredient, you can create a completely new and delicious meal. In the next few pages, I'll show you my favorite ways to make last night's dinner into today's brand-new best meal ever. It's even more delicious the next day, and I'm willing to bet that you, too, will be transformed into a lover of leftovers.

Pack Your Bowl

When I'm working from home, I use leftovers most frequently for lunch—it's easy to throw a variety of salads into a bowl while I'm on a call to make an incredible meal. I'll often create one or two new elements to add into the mix, but it's usually quite simple, like sliced cucumber or carrot, the addition of sauerkraut, or a leftover grain like rice or farro. Use the leftovers in your fridge to make it your own.

7 min egg
(page 40)

bulgur

taco slaw
(page 32)

confetti greens
(page 13)

crispy tofu
(page 27)

gg chicken salad
(page 78)

tomatoes

carrots

sesame cucs
(page 207)

purple slaw
(page 81)

Toasts

I love toast as a vessel for leftovers. Most often, I pan-fry a slice of sourdough in olive oil, sprinkle it with salt and pepper, and then rub a clove of garlic on the bread while it's still hot. Spread cottage cheese, avocado, or hummus on top so the salad has something to stick to, and top with a big scoop of whatever salad you've got. Here are a few of my favorites to get you started.

cabbage slaw on chicken salad sesame cues
(pages 35, 78, 272)

purple beet slaw + ricotta cheese
(page 81)

confetti greens (page 13)
avocado tomatoes + cottage cheese

7 min egg (page 40)
avocado + green goddess sauce
(page 78)

Veggies & Eggs

VEGETARIAN, GLUTEN-FREE

15 minutes | Serves 1 to 2

This is one of my favorite ways to use leftovers around 10:00 a.m. when I'm hungry and working from home. I find finishing all the leftovers so thrilling, and putting an egg on top transforms last night's dinner into something entirely new. (Leftover Chinese food is even better for breakfast when prepared this way.)

This recipe checks so many boxes; it's nourishing, a way to use your leftovers (or whatever you've got lying around) as an ingredient, and so quick and easy to throw together.

A few slices leftover roasted sweet potato

1 cup leftover steamed broccoli and/or asparagus (you can use any steamed veggies for this!)

1 sweet red pepper

1 tablespoon avocado oil

1 garlic clove, grated with a Microplane

Fine sea salt and black pepper

2 large eggs

1 ripe avocado

1. Chop the sweet potatoes, broccoli, and pepper into small pieces.

2. Heat the avocado oil in a medium or large frying pan over medium heat and add the veggies.

3. Add the garlic into the veggies and stir everything together. Season with salt and pepper and cook for a few minutes, just to warm everything through.

4. Make a well in the veggies with the back of a spatula and crack the eggs into the well. Season the eggs with salt and pepper. Lower the heat and cover, just until the tops of the eggs are opaque, about 2 minutes.

5. Transfer the veggies to a plate and top with the sliced avocado. Season with salt and pepper. Serve immediately.

Tip

We always keep avocados on hand to add to quick meals like this one. Make sure to buy the ones with the nub still on top, and if they're hard, leave them out on the counter until you can make a thumbprint in the top. Once that happens, move it to the fridge until you're ready to eat.

Leftovers Soup

Poaching an egg right in leftover soup is a great way to make your soup extra filling, especially if it doesn't already have protein in it. Bring leftover soup to a simmer on the stove, crack an egg in, and let it cook until the egg whites are cooked but the yolk is still runny (about 3 minutes). The yolk combines with the broth to create a silky texture that's out of this world. Once the egg is cooked, serve immediately. You won't believe you're eating leftovers.

Put an Egg on It

I love an egg on leftovers, in a bowl, on toast, or over a salad. They're one of my go-tos because you can make them in advance and keep them in the fridge for a hearty meal. Master your eggs—it makes everything easier.

1. Bring a large pot of water to a boil and add the egg. Prepare an ice bath.

2. How long you cook it depends on how runny you want your yolk—6 minutes for just-set whites and a runny yolk, 9 minutes for firm whites and slightly jammy yolk, and 11 minutes for hard-boiled.

3. Transfer the eggs to an ice bath once time is up to stop the cooking. Let cool completely. Crack open immediately or store in the fridge to have the best protein around on demand.

6 min

9 min

11 min

sides & snacks

Categorizing every recipe of this book into separate sections turned out to be one of the hardest parts of the writing process. And I'm okay with telling you that's why this somehow became the miscellaneous section. There are so many recipes I love and have been making for years that didn't have a perfect home in the book, but they needed to be included. These recipes are woven into the fabric of my life and my home. When I tell my kids or a friend to come eat, it could be Wings (page 217) fresh out of the oven or Movie Night Popcorn (page 235) covered in all my favorite flavors. These are recipes that are easy, delicious—and, while not meals individually, could be combined into the most amazing meal.

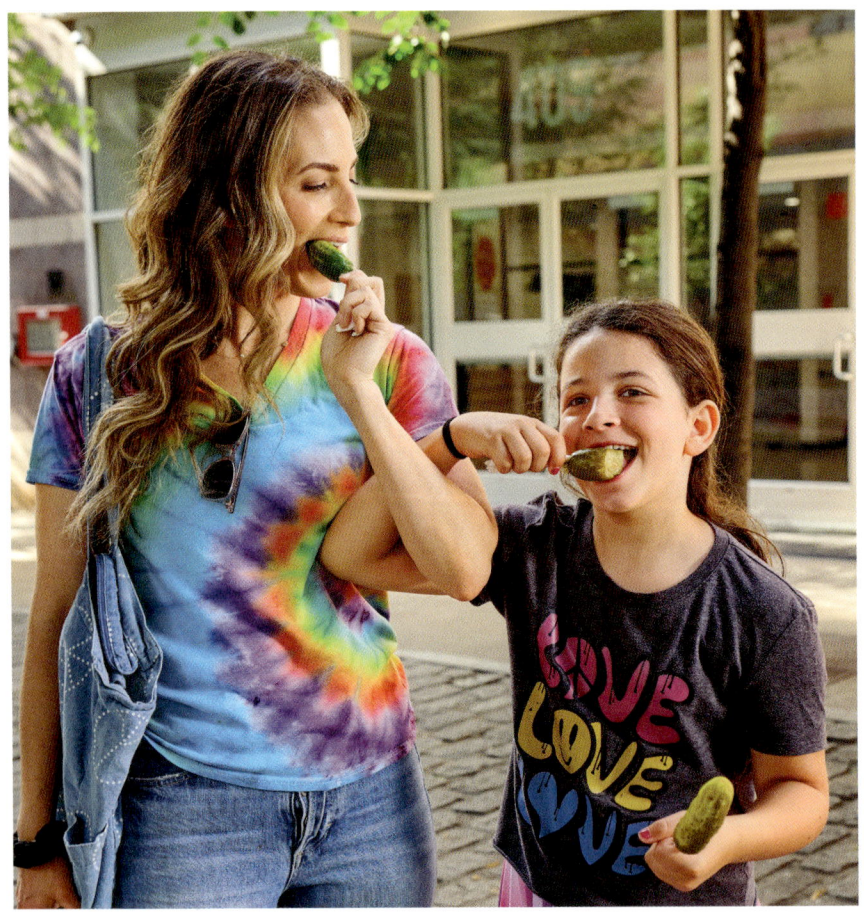

Snacks are intended to be eaten in between meals as a way to give you nourishment and/or fulfillment when your body craves it. They don't need to hit all the notes of a meal (protein, green, grain), but they should give you energy and make you feel good. These are the smaller dishes I make when I'm hungry or friends stop by. I serve them as soon as they're ready, and everybody gathers around to enjoy. I hope you do, too.

New Pickles

VEGAN, GLUTEN-FREE

5 minutes active, 48 hours total | Makes 6 pickles

One day, we were waiting in line at Picklelicious at the farmers market and ran into my daughter's friend Clara, who was eating a pickle on a stick. That was the day my daughter finally decided to try one—and the day she finally decided she loves pickles. Now, she'll eat a wide variety of pickles, but new pickles were the first type she loved. New pickles are milder than others because they're fermented for a short time period. This keeps them bright green and crunchy. We could only ever find them at the farmers market, which meant I had to learn how to make them. It was impossible to find a recipe online. Eventually, I found an article that explained how they were made, so I tried over and over again until I got the ratios just right. They're such a good, easy, and underrated pickle. And if you've never tried them, now's your chance.

1½ tablespoons fine sea salt
7 garlic cloves
6 Persian cucumbers

1. Fill a 32-ounce jar halfway with filtered water.

2. Add the salt, garlic, and whole cucumbers to the jar. It should be totally full and the cucumbers submerged. Fill the jar with more water if needed.

3. Shake the jar and let sit in the fridge for 48 hours. Eat plain, or use to make Tuna Salad (page 74) or Green Goddess Chicken Salad (page 78). Use within 2 weeks.

Tzatziki

VEGETARIAN, GLUTEN-FREE

15 minutes | Makes 1½ cups

Make tzatziki from scratch one time and you'll never buy it premade again. The first tzatziki I fell in love with was at Ali Baba, a Turkish restaurant in New York City on Thirty-Fourth Street between Second and Third Avenues. Then I'd buy it all the time at Whole Foods after Adi and I moved in together. Once I discovered a recipe, I realized how simple it was and never looked back. It's so easy, and you can adapt the flavors to taste exactly how you want it. I like to grate the cucumbers so you don't have chunks and squeeze all the moisture out of them for a thicker consistency.

1½ cups full-fat plain Greek yogurt
3 mini cucumbers
2 garlic cloves, grated with a Microplane
1 lemon
½ teaspoon fine sea salt

1. Put the yogurt in a small bowl.

2. Grate one cucumber using the wide holes of a box grater and place on a towel. Squeeze out the excess moisture, then add it to the bowl with the yogurt.

3. Add the garlic and lemon juice to the bowl and stir together. Season with the salt, taste, and adjust seasoning as needed.

4. Slice the remaining cucumbers into ½-inch pieces on a bias and serve with the tzatziki. Store any leftovers in an airtight container in the fridge for 3 to 5 days.

 Tip Whenever you go to a Mediterranean or Greek restaurant, ask for sliced cucumbers with whatever dips you order. It's a great way to enjoy the entire spread without filling up quickly on pita.

Sesame Cukes

VEGAN, GLUTEN-FREE

15 minutes | Serves 2

This salad was inspired by an appetizer I had at Ippudo, one of my favorite ramen spots, near Union Square—I immediately picked up a bag of gochugaru at the market on my way home and made it the next day. You could put the cukes on top of a sandwich or eat them as a light and refreshing snack.

I love an excuse to make a salad with only cucumbers because they're so versatile. The flavor isn't overpowering, and they're crunchy and refreshing. In *Come Hungry*, I shared one of my favorites, a finely chopped dilly cucumber salad. Here's another simple way to make a salad when you have only cucumbers in the fridge.

3 mini cucumbers

1 tablespoon toasted sesame oil

1 tablespoon rice vinegar

½ teaspoon fine sea salt

1 teaspoon garlic powder

Juice of ½ lime (about 1 tablespoon)

2 garlic cloves, grated

2 teaspoons sesame seeds, plus more for garnish

Gochugaru, to garnish

Flaky sea salt, to garnish

1. Slice the cucumbers into ½-inch rounds on the bias. Transfer them to a large bowl and add the sesame oil, vinegar, salt, garlic powder, lime juice, garlic cloves, and sesame seeds and stir gently to combine.

2. Plate the dressed cucumbers and drizzle with any extra dressing in the bowl.

3. Top with gochugaru, flaky sea salt, and sesame seeds to taste. Serve immediately.

Gochugaru

Gochugaru is a milder chili flake from Korea. It's often used in kimchis and Korean barbecue dishes. You can find it in the spice section at grocery stores and in larger quantities at Asian markets; I got mine at the farmers market. I love to use it to add extra flavor and color without a ton of heat. You know I don't do spicy!

String Beans with Almonds & Tahini

VEGAN, GLUTEN-FREE

20 minutes | Serves 2 to 4

A few years ago, Adi and I went to Anguilla for a long weekend without the kids. One of our most memorable meals was at Blanchards—a world-renowned Caribbean restaurant right on the beach. We couldn't decide what to order because there were so many veggie-packed dishes on the menu and it all sounded incredible. In true Melissa and Adi fashion, we decided to order one of everything we wanted, and ended up eating it all.

As soon as I laid eyes on it, I knew I had to re-create a version of this dish when I got home—simple sautéed veg drizzled with an incredible vinaigrette and roasted cashews. This isn't exactly the same, but every time I make it, it takes me back to Anguilla with my wonderful husband and the delicious meal we ate by the sea.

12 ounces green beans

⅓ cup sliced almonds

Juice of 1½ lemons (just under ½ cup)

2 garlic cloves, grated and divided

¼ cup extra virgin olive oil

1 teaspoon fine sea salt

Black pepper

¼ cup tahini

1. Bring a large pot of water to a boil over high heat.

2. Trim the beans to remove the pointy ends and add the beans to the boiling water. Cook for 1½ minutes, then drain and transfer directly to a plate.

3. At the same time, heat a small frying pan over medium heat and add the almonds. Cook, tossing occasionally, until golden and fragrant, 3 to 5 minutes.

4. Whisk together 3 tablespoons of the lemon juice, 1 grated garlic clove, the olive oil, ½ teaspoon of the salt, and a few turns of pepper in a small bowl.

5. Pour the dressing over the green beans and mix well to combine.

6. In another bowl, whisk together the tahini and remaining lemon juice. Add water, 1 teaspoon at a time. It will be thick, then thin again. Add water until the tahini is pourable. Stir in the remaining grated garlic clove and ½ teaspoon salt.

7. Top the green beans with the almonds and drizzle with the tahini just before serving. Store any leftovers in an airtight container in the fridge for 3 to 5 days. (If you don't plan to serve it all at once, try to keep the tahini and green beans separate.)

Hummus

VEGAN, GLUTEN-FREE

25 minutes | Makes 2 cups

Adi and I use hummus and tahini as condiments the way most people use ketchup, mustard, and mayonnaise. You can't be married to an Israeli and not know how to make hummus. When we first started dating, I quickly learned that he puts hummus on everything, and in no time, I learned how to make it. There are a few tricks to ensure a smooth, creamy hummus, like boiling your chickpeas with baking soda and using ice water to make it smooth. You can serve it with chopped tomatoes and cucumbers drizzled in olive oil, or you can serve it plain. It's great to keep in the fridge to spread on a sandwich or eat as a snack between meals.

½ teaspoon baking soda
One 15.5-ounce can chickpeas, drained
½ cup tahini paste
Juice of 1 lemon (about 3 tablespoons)
¾ teaspoon fine sea salt, plus more to season
1 large garlic clove, grated
Ice water
¼ to ½ teaspoon cumin
Black pepper
Extra virgin olive oil, to drizzle

1. Boil a large pot of water and add the baking soda. Add the chickpeas and cook until they get plump and the skin starts to come off, about 20 minutes. Drain and rinse the chickpeas.

2. Add the tahini, lemon juice, and ½ teaspoon of the salt to the bowl of a food processor and pulse to combine. Add the garlic and 2 to 3 tablespoons ice water, then blend again.

3. Transfer the chickpeas to the food processor and process until smooth. Season with the cumin, the remaining ¼ teaspoon salt, and pepper, adjusting seasonings to taste.

4. Place a large spoonful of hummus in a low-rimmed bowl or plate and use the spoon to swirl around the middle. Drizzle with olive oil, salt, and pepper. Serve immediately or store in an airtight container in the fridge for up to 5 days.

Ranch Dip

VEGETARIAN, GLUTEN-FREE

10 minutes | Makes 2 cups

I love ranch dressing. I used to eat it all the time as a kid with sliced cucumbers and carrots. In almost all of the recipes I create, I focus on making them equally nutritious and delicious, so you can eat as much as you want. This one fits that bill and is a family favorite. It's packed with all the classic ranch flavors: onion, dill, and chives, with a creamy base. And because the creaminess comes from cottage cheese, it's also filled with protein. It's so easy to make, you can whip it up in no time.

One 16-ounce container whole-milk cottage cheese

¼ cup fresh dill

¼ cup fresh chives

¼ cup fresh parsley

1 teaspoon garlic powder

Juice of 1 lemon (about 3 tablespoons)

¼ teaspoon black pepper

½ teaspoon fine sea salt

Carrots, cucumbers, radishes, or any other crudité, plus pita or pita chips, to serve

1. Combine the cottage cheese, dill, chives, parsley, garlic powder, lemon juice, pepper, and salt in a food processor and pulse until smooth. Don't overblend—you should still see specks of green in the dip.

2. Serve immediately with crudité and/or pita or pita chips. Store any leftovers in an airtight container in the fridge for up to 3 days. If the dip separates in the fridge, stir before serving.

Sesame Peas

VEGAN, GLUTEN-FREE

15 minutes | Serves 4

When sugar snap peas are in season, I eat them as often as possible. At the farmers market, I buy two containers—one for salads and one for dinner recipes for the week ahead. And I love snacking on them raw, or sautéed, like in this recipe. I try not to cook them for too long, to keep the crunch. The sauce here is the star of the show—it perfectly elevates the already delicious vegetable. (It's great on green beans, too.)

2 cups sugar snap peas

3 garlic cloves, grated

1½ teaspoons minced ginger

Juice of ½ lime (about 1 tablespoon), plus more for garnish

1 tablespoon avocado oil

¼ teaspoon black pepper

¼ teaspoon gochugaru

1 teaspoon fine sea salt

1 teaspoon sesame seeds, plus more for garnish

1 teaspoon sesame oil, plus more for garnish

1. Trim the snap peas and remove the string (it should easily pull off).

2. Whisk together the garlic, ginger, lime juice, and avocado oil in a small bowl.

3. Heat a large frying pan over medium-high heat. Add the snap peas to the pan and cover with the dressing. Toss to evenly combine and cook until bright green, with some golden brown, 5 minutes.

4. Stir in the pepper, gochugaru, and salt. Stir occasionally, until slightly toasted.

5. Remove the peas from the pan after 5 minutes and garnish with more sesame seeds, a squeeze of lime juice, and a drizzle of sesame oil. Store any leftovers in an airtight container in the fridge for 3 to 5 days.

Wings

GLUTEN-FREE

45 minutes | Serves 4

My mom and my aunt love wings. I remember sitting across the table from my mom when I was little and watching her enjoy the wing of the Oven Stuffer she prepared for dinner, just nibbling away until she got down to the bones. It looked so fun. That's a large part of why I love wings so much, and now my daughter does, too! It's like a game to eat them—let's see who can get the bones the cleanest—and they are oh so delicious. This is a foolproof recipe that uses a combination of some of my favorite spices. It's a great snack to set out while you watch the game or to serve when you have friends over.

1 tablespoon sweet paprika
1 teaspoon garlic powder
1 teaspoon fine sea salt
½ teaspoon turmeric
¼ teaspoon black pepper
Pinch of cayenne pepper (optional)
1¾ pounds whole chicken wings, at room temperature
2 teaspoons avocado oil

1. Preheat the oven to 500°F.

2. In a large bowl, whisk together the paprika, garlic powder, salt, turmeric, and pepper. If you want to make the wings spicy, add the cayenne pepper.

3. Dry off the chicken wings with a paper towel and add them to the bowl. Use your hands to get them fully coated in the spice rub.

4. Drizzle the avocado oil over the chicken wings and use your hands to get them evenly coated.

5. Place the wings on an unlined baking sheet in an even layer and bake for 35 minutes. The internal temperature will reach 165°F much sooner than that, but I like to cook them longer so the outside is crispy. Store any leftovers in an airtight container in the fridge for 3 to 5 days. Reheat at 375°F for 10 to 15 minutes.

Roasted Veggie Dip

VEGAN, GLUTEN-FREE

1 hour 20 minutes | Makes 2 cups

Adi and his mom make dishes like this all the time, especially when they're hosting. This one is inspired by a similar dip I included in *Come Hungry*, but this time, I've added soft, roasted onion, tomato, tahini, and even more garlic. The method of making this is so fun—you chop all the softened vegetables on a cutting board until the dip comes together, seasoning and adding elements as you go. It's incredible as a dip, but you can also use it to spread over a pita with Chicken Schnitzel (page 159). If you want to serve this dip at a party, make it the day before, but be prepared to not have any leftovers once people leave.

1 medium eggplant

1½ teaspoons fine sea salt, plus more to taste

1 yellow onion

1 large tomato

1 head garlic, plus 1 garlic clove

1 red bell pepper

Avocado oil spray

Black pepper

Juice of ½ lemon (about 1½ tablespoons)

2 tablespoons chopped fresh parsley, plus more to garnish

3 tablespoons tahini

Extra virgin olive oil

1. Preheat the oven to 450°F and line a baking sheet with parchment paper.

2. Slice the eggplant in half lengthwise and score the flesh. Sprinkle each side with ¼ teaspoon salt and place, flesh-side down, on the baking sheet.

3. Cut the onion and tomato in half and add to the baking sheet. Place the head of garlic and bell pepper on the baking sheet as well.

4. Coat the veggies with avocado oil spray and season with ¼ teaspoon salt and a few turns of pepper.

5. Roast all the veggies for 30 to 35 minutes, until the skin on the pepper has blackened and the garlic is soft. Remove the pepper from the tray carefully (tongs make this easier) and place in a glass container with a lid to cool.

6. Return the eggplant to the oven and continue baking for an additional 30 minutes, until the flesh is completely soft and the exterior is slightly charred.

continued

7. Once the pepper has cooled, peel the skin off (this should be easy), remove the seeds, and slice, reserving the oil and juices. Keep the pepper slices on your cutting board.

8. Once the eggplant is cool enough to handle, scoop out the eggplant flesh and place on the cutting board with the pepper, along with the onion and tomato. Carefully squeeze the roasted garlic out onto the board.

9. Using a sharp knife, finely chop all the veggies until it starts to form a thick, dip-like consistency. Squeeze the lemon juice onto the mixture, using your knife to fold it in.

10. Grate the remaining garlic clove with a Microplane into the paste, then season with ½ teaspoon salt. Taste and add more salt as needed.

11. Add the parsley and tahini to the dip and fold them in, mixing well until combined.

12. Transfer to a shallow bowl and top with a sprinkle of parsley and a drizzle of olive oil for garnish. Store in an airtight container in the fridge for 3 to 5 days.

Roasted Cauliflower

VEGAN, GLUTEN-FREE

1 hour 30 minutes | Serves 2 to 4

I see whole-roasted cauliflowers on Instagram all the time. They're gorgeous, but in my experience, I don't like that the seasoning is only on the outside. I prefer to cut my cauliflower into quarters so I can cover it all over with a delicious spice blend. If you bake it for the right amount of time at the right temperature, you'll get the perfect texture: crispy on the outside and soft on the inside. Flip it halfway through to get delicious crispy edges. You've never tasted cauliflower so good!

1 head cauliflower

¼ cup plus 1 teaspoon avocado oil

5 garlic cloves, grated

1 teaspoon fine sea salt, plus more to taste

1 teaspoon sweet paprika

1 teaspoon turmeric

2 teaspoons za'atar

1 teaspoon garlic powder

Black pepper

1. Preheat the oven to 400°F and line a baking sheet with parchment paper.

2. Wash the cauliflower and trim off the bottom of the stem and the excess leaves. Cut into quarters. It's okay if a few florets fall off, but try to keep as much of it intact as possible.

3. In a small bowl, whisk together ¼ cup of the avocado oil, the garlic, salt, paprika, turmeric, za'atar, garlic powder, and a few turns of pepper until well combined.

4. Coat the cauliflower with the spice mixture using your hands or a brush to get every nook coated. Really get in there!

5. Season with a pinch of salt and pepper, drizzle the remaining 1 teaspoon avocado oil over the cauliflower, and place on the baking sheet.

6. Roast the cauliflower for 1 hour, until tender. Serve immediately; store leftovers in an airtight container in the fridge for up to 4 days.

7-Minute Cauliflower

VEGAN, GLUTEN-FREE

45 minutes | Serves 2 to 4

Whenever I don't have time to invest in roasting perfectly crispy cauliflower, I make this instead. When you chop cauliflower into small pieces, boil it, and cover it in delicious dressing, you get an incredible side in just seven minutes. Like the Whole Roasted Eggplant (page 227), it's important to coat the cauliflower in the dressing while it's still warm, to bloom the aromatics.

1 head cauliflower
2 garlic cloves, grated
3 tablespoons freshly chopped chives
1 tablespoon fresh parsley
1 tablespoon fresh oregano
¼ cup extra virgin olive oil
¼ teaspoon black pepper
Juice of 1 lemon (about 3 tablespoons)
2 tablespoons nutritional yeast
2 teaspoons za'atar
1 tablespoon sesame seeds
1 teaspoon fine sea salt

1. Boil a large pot of water over high heat.

2. Remove the core from the cauliflower and chop the head into small florets (1 inch or smaller).

3. Add the cauliflower to the boiling water and cook until the florets are al dente, about 7 minutes. They shouldn't be too soft.

4. While the cauliflower cooks, add the garlic, chives, parsley, oregano, olive oil, pepper, lemon juice, nutritional yeast, za'atar, sesame seeds, and salt to a large bowl. Whisk well to combine. Taste and adjust the seasonings as needed.

5. Drain the cauliflower and transfer it directly to the bowl of aromatics. The heat will help the flavors bloom.

6. Stir well to coat the cauliflower in dressing. Serve immediately or store in the fridge in an airtight container until ready to serve. Eat within 3 to 5 days.

Whole Roasted Eggplant

VEGAN, GLUTEN-FREE

45 minutes | Serves 2 to 4

Consider this recipe a gift from Mother Nature: You don't need much to make something incredibly delicious. The key to getting the best result with this eggplant is making sure it's cooked through and preparing it right out of the oven, while it's piping-hot. The heat helps bloom the flavors of the garlic and herbs, which combine with the juices to create a truly delicious side. When you think you have nothing to make and spot an eggplant in the back of your produce drawer, make this dish.

1 medium eggplant, washed

3 to 4 scallions, trimmed and cut into ¼-inch pieces

¼ cup chopped parsley or cilantro

¼ cup tahini

Juice of 1 lemon (about 3 tablespoons)

1 garlic clove, grated

½ teaspoon fine sea salt

1 jalapeño, sliced (optional)

1. Preheat the oven to broil and position the oven rack on the top setting. Poke the eggplant all over with the tines of a fork and place on a sheet pan. Broil on high for 10 minutes, then flip and broil for another 10 to 15 minutes. Remove the eggplant from the oven when it can no longer hold its shape, the skin is wrinkly, and it starts to smell a bit like a campfire. That's the flavor!

2. In a small bowl, stir together the scallions and parsley.

3. Whisk together the tahini and lemon juice. Add water, 1 tablespoon at a time—it will be thick, then thin out—until it's pourable and slightly thinner than mustard. Stir in the garlic and salt and adjust the seasonings to taste.

4. Once the eggplant is cool enough to handle—but still hot—cut it in half lengthwise.

5. Drizzle the eggplant generously with the tahini mixture and sprinkle the herbs on top to serve. Add a few slices of jalapeño if you want a little spice. Enjoy immediately.

Stuffed Artichokes

VEGETARIAN

45 minutes | Serves 4

There's a tiny, cash-only restaurant in Hoboken called Augustino's that we love to go to. It's family-run and smaller than my living room, so we have to plan ahead and make a reservation. Augustino's has the best stuffed artichokes. Whenever we go there for dinner, we each order our own so we don't have to share. One day, my oldest told me she wanted to try stuffed artichokes—I have no idea what prompted it—so I made them for her based on the artichokes we knew and loved. They were a hit, and now she requests them all the time.

Artichokes can seem intimidating at first. They're big and require some pruning before they're edible. If you've never made them before, I hope this recipe demystifies the process for you and becomes an instant family favorite, like it is in our house.

4 whole artichokes

1½ cups breadcrumbs

3 garlic cloves, grated

1 teaspoon fine sea salt

¼ teaspoon black pepper

1 tablespoon fresh oregano

Juice of ½ lemon (about 1½ tablespoons)

½ cup freshly grated Parmesan, plus more to top

2 to 3 tablespoons extra virgin olive oil

1 cup vegetable broth

½ cup white wine

1. Use a large serrated knife to cut the tops off the artichokes and cut the points off the leaves with kitchen shears. Cut ½ inch off the stem and peel to remove the stem's fibrous exterior.

2. Place a steamer basket in a large pot and bring 2 inches of water to a boil. Add the artichokes to the steamer basket and cover, keeping the heat on medium. Steam until the artichokes are tender, about 30 minutes.

3. While the artichokes steam, combine the breadcrumbs, garlic, salt, pepper, oregano, lemon juice, and Parmesan in a large bowl. Add the olive oil, 1 tablespoon at a time, until the mixture looks like wet sand.

4. Preheat the oven to 350°F.

5. Once the artichokes are steamed, transfer them to a rectangular casserole dish.

6. Stuff each artichoke with equal parts stuffing (about ⅓ cup per artichoke).

7. Pour the broth and wine into the bottom of the casserole dish and top the artichokes with any remaining breadcrumb mixture.

8. Sprinkle extra Parmesan on top and bake for 45 to 50 minutes, until the tops are golden brown. Best enjoyed immediately.

Sautéed Bok Choy

VEGAN, GLUTEN-FREE*

15 minutes | Serves 2 to 4

If you follow me on social media, you know I love bok choy. It's great raw as the base of a salad (like 11) and is even more delicious when you sauté it. The flavor combination of sesame oil, tamari, garlic, and ginger is one of my all-time faves. This recipe is an easy place to start if you're new to the kitchen. It's great served over rice and with protein on top if you want to make it a meal.

2 heads bok choy

1 tablespoon tamari

3 garlic cloves, grated

2 teaspoons freshly grated ginger (about one 2-inch knob)

1 tablespoon sesame seeds, plus more for garnish

2 tablespoons avocado oil

¼ teaspoon fine sea salt

¼ teaspoon black pepper

Juice of 1 lemon cheek (about 2 teaspoons)

1 tablespoon sesame oil

1. Wash and dry the bok choy well and stack the leaves. Cut down the middle lengthwise, then cut into ¾-inch pieces.

2. In a small bowl, whisk together the tamari, garlic, ginger, and sesame seeds to make a paste.

3. Heat the avocado oil in a large pan over medium heat, then add the bok choy.

4. Season with salt and pepper and let the bok choy wilt slightly, about 1 minute.

5. Add the paste to the pan and cook until the bok choy leaves are fully wilted, 3 to 5 minutes more.

6. Remove the pan from heat and squeeze the lemon cheek over it, and drizzle with the sesame oil.

7. Garnish with sesame seeds and serve as a side or on toast. Store any leftovers in an airtight container in the fridge for 3 to 5 days.

 To make this gluten-free, make sure to use GF-certified tamari.

Sautéed Cabbage

VEGETARIAN, GLUTEN-FREE

20 minutes | Serves 4 as a side

When I was little, my maternal grandfather, Grandpa Sammy, would tell us stories about growing up during the Great Depression and eating lots of potatoes, onions, and cabbage. He lived in a tenement on the Lower East Side with his parents and six sisters, playing stickball on the corner of Essex and Rivington Streets near the old Essex Market. His father sold fruit on the street from a cart. I can't help but think of Grandpa Sammy when I make simple dishes like this one. It's so easy—it's really just cabbage and onions—and is a great way to use that cabbage you forgot about back in the fridge that's somehow still good. Food is how I connect with people in the past and present, and I love remembering my grandpa as I twirl cabbage around my fork. He would love it.

2 tablespoons avocado oil

1 yellow onion

4 large garlic cloves, roughly chopped

½ teaspoon fine sea salt

1 green cabbage

Juice of ½ lemon (about 1½ tablespoons)

1 tablespoon tamari (optional)

1 tablespoon toasted sesame oil (optional)

Sesame seeds, for garnish

1. Heat the avocado oil in a large pan over medium-high heat.

2. Thinly slice the onion and add to the pan. Cook until slightly translucent, 2 to 3 minutes, then add the garlic.

3. Lower the heat to medium-low so the garlic doesn't burn.

4. Add the salt and let cook while you cut the cabbage.

5. Cut the cabbage into ¼-inch slices and add them to the pan. Cook for 5 to 6 minutes, stirring occasionally so the cabbage wilts but keeps its crunch.

6. Stir in the lemon juice and transfer the cabbage to a bowl.

7. Add the tamari and toasted sesame oil, if using, and top with sesame seeds. Serve immediately. Store any leftovers in an airtight container in the fridge for up to 4 days.

Movie Night Popcorn

VEGAN, GLUTEN-FREE

5 minutes | Serves 4

When we have movie nights, the kids pick the movie and Adi makes the popcorn. He knows to make me my own bowl because my kids get annoyed with me taking handfuls of theirs. A few years ago, I made this spice blend to put on top of it, and it's truly addictive. It's cheesy (but vegan!), with all my favorite flavor profiles—garlic, oregano, and sweet paprika. I spray the popcorn with avocado oil so the powder sticks to it. It reminds me of the popcorn I grew up eating as a kid but with good-for-you ingredients—the best of both worlds. Make a big batch of the spice blend to keep on hand for movie nights. It's also great on pumpkin seeds and added to simple vinaigrette.

4½ cups plain popped popcorn
Avocado oil spray
2 tablespoons nutritional yeast
1 tablespoon dried oregano
2 teaspoons fine sea salt
½ teaspoon black pepper
1 tablespoon garlic powder

1. Spray the popcorn with avocado oil spray and toss to evenly coat.

2. Whisk the nutritional yeast, oregano, salt, pepper, and garlic powder together in a small bowl and sprinkle a few teaspoons over the popcorn.

3. Gently mix to combine and enjoy immediately. Save any remaining seasoning in an airtight container at room temperature for next time. Use within six months for optimal flavor.

dessert

After every meal, I crave a bite of something sweet. That's why Baked by Melissa exists—it's the perfect bite at the end of the meal. If I don't have anything else, oftentimes I'll finish dinner and go into my pantry to get a handful of dark chocolate chips. Other times, I'll see what ingredients we have to whip something up. Sometimes I make dessert by myself, and sometimes my kids help. For me, it's all about the process. When my kids were little—too little to understand what was happening—I'd make sugar cookies with them as my own creative outlet.

Now, they're the ones asking if we can make dessert. The answer is always yes.

This section is filled with a variety of recipes—some are sweetened with dates, some sneak veggies in, and others are filled with leftover chocolate candy. They're all main-stays in my house. Like in every other chapter in this book, these are the tried-and-true recipes I make for my family over and over again. I hope they find their way into your dessert rotation, too, and give you an excuse to spend time in the kitchen with people you love. There's really nothing sweeter.

Brown Butter Candy Cookies

30 minutes active, up to 24 hours inactive | Makes 36 cookies

This recipe is our family's favorite Halloween tradition. Every year when we get home from trick-or-treating, my kids and I run to the kitchen to make these cookies while still in costume. I love any excuse to get my kids in the kitchen with me, and they love to open all the individual candies. It's a great way to use Halloween candy—or any candy you have left over from a party or goody bag—in a more productive way. Everyone loves these cookies. I highly recommend you make them all year-round.

1 cup (2 sticks) unsalted butter

¾ cup granulated sugar

¾ cup light brown sugar, packed

2 large eggs

2 teaspoons vanilla extract or paste

2¼ cups all-purpose flour

1 teaspoon baking soda

1 teaspoon fine sea salt

2 cups chocolate candy, chopped (M&Ms, Milky Way, Reeses, Snickers, etc.! You can also add pretzel pieces for crunch/salt), plus more for topping

Flaky sea salt, for topping

1. In a medium saucepan, melt the butter over medium heat and swirl occasionally until brown specks form, 5 to 7 minutes. Once these specks appear and the butter smells slightly nutty, remove from the heat and let cool to room temperature. Don't walk away, as it can burn quickly.

2. Combine the butter and sugars in the bowl of a stand mixer and, using the paddle attachment, beat on medium-high speed until light and fluffy, 3 to 5 minutes.

3. Add the eggs, one at a time, mixing between each addition, followed by the vanilla.

4. Mix in the flour, baking soda, and salt, and stir on medium-low until a dough forms.

5. Fold the candy into the dough until just combined, being careful not to overmix. Place the mixing bowl in the fridge to chill for at least 30 minutes or up to 24 hours. Chilling helps the cookies bake more evenly. If you're in a rush you can skip this step, but I highly recommend it.

continued

6. Preheat the oven to 350°F and line a baking sheet with parchment paper.

7. Remove the chilled dough from the fridge and let sit for 5 to 10 minutes so it's pliable. Scoop the dough onto the baking sheet and top each ball with additional candy or chocolate chips.

8. Bake for 12 minutes, until lightly golden.

9. Immediately after you remove the cookies from the oven, swirl a large glass or biscuit cutter around them to get a perfect circle.

10. Top with flaky sea salt and try not to eat them all at once. Store in an airtight container at room temperature for 3 days.

Tip Freeze portioned cookie dough balls on a baking sheet, then transfer to a freezer-safe bag. When you want a cookie, bring the dough balls to room temperature and bake at 350°F for 12 minutes.

Date Balls

VEGAN, GLUTEN-FREE

20 minutes | Makes 2 dozen balls

When I have date balls in the fridge, it gives me something to look forward to after dinner. They're one of those really special treats that make you feel satisfied and nourished at the same time, made with simple, whole ingredients. And better yet, they're so easy to make. You can sub any nuts or seeds you have. It's all about the consistency—you're going for a Play-Doh-like texture that's easy to roll into balls. You can add cocoa powder to make chocolate balls, add chocolate chips, or roll them in coconut. Any way you make them, they're the perfect pick-me-up.

14 ounces medjool dates, pitted
⅓ cup raw, unsalted cashews
⅓ cup unsalted walnuts
⅓ cup unsweetened coconut flakes
¼ cup pumpkin seeds
¼ cup hemp seeds
2 teaspoons vanilla paste
1 teaspoon cinnamon
1 teaspoon fine sea salt
Flaky sea salt
¼ cup cocoa powder (optional)

1. Pulse the dates, cashews, walnuts, coconut, pumpkin seeds, hemp seeds, vanilla, cinnamon, and fine sea salt together in a food processor until it reaches a Play-Doh-like consistency.

2. Roll the mixture into 1-inch balls and sprinkle with flaky sea salt.

3. Store in an airtight container in the fridge for up to 1 week.

Granola Bars

GLUTEN-FREE, VEGETARIAN*

1 hour 45 minutes (including cooling time) | Makes 18 rectangular granola bars

Out of all the dessert recipes in this book, I've made these the most. I've been making them for my kids their entire lives. They're so delicious and filled with good stuff that, miraculously, my kids love to eat. Sometimes I even find them hidden in my youngest's desk. I whip up a batch any time we travel to take on the plane, and I pack them in school lunches. The best part is the inclusions are entirely customizable. You can use whatever nuts, seeds, and chocolate you want. This is also a favorite recipe among all my mom friends. They're so easy, and once you get the hang of it, you can have a batch ready in just a few minutes.

3 cups rolled oats

½ cup pumpkin seeds

½ cup sliced almonds

¼ cup sesame seeds

1 cup chocolate chips

¼ cup extra virgin olive oil

⅓ cup tahini or other nut butter

½ cup honey

1 teaspoon vanilla paste or extract

½ teaspoon fine sea salt

Flaky sea salt

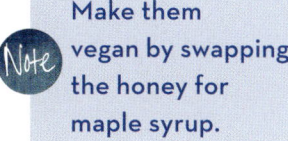

Note Make them vegan by swapping the honey for maple syrup.

1. Preheat the oven to 350°F and line a 9 × 9-inch square pan with parchment paper.

2. Combine the oats, pumpkin seeds, almonds, sesame seeds, and chocolate chips in a large bowl.

3. In a separate bowl, combine the olive oil, tahini, honey, vanilla, and fine sea salt.

4. Pour the wet ingredients into the dry mixture and use your hands to evenly coat.

5. Push the granola mixture into the prepared pan, using parchment paper to make it flat without sticking to your hands.

6. Sprinkle the top with flaky sea salt.

7. Bake for 28 to 30 minutes, until the edges are golden. Keep an eye on them—as soon as the edges start to turn golden, take them out.

8. Cool to room temperature, then remove the granola from the pan and pop in the fridge for 1 hour to completely cool—you have to let them cool all the way before cutting or they'll fall apart.

9. Cut the cooled granola into squares or bars and wrap in parchment paper. Keep the wrapped granola bars in an airtight container at room temperature for up to 1 week.

Pumpkin Doughnut Muffins

45 minutes | Makes 12 muffins

This recipe is an 11/10 thanks to one secret ingredient: mace. Mace is similar to nutmeg, with a warm, complex flavor. I don't like nutmeg, but I do like mace, so if you're the same, don't let that deter you. When you add mace to cake, it gives it a distinct doughnut flavor. (Don't tell anyone, but that's how we make our doughnut flavor at Baked by Melissa.) When you combine mace with pumpkin, it creates the most moist, fluffy cake that is out of this world. And oh my god, the crumble—make it once and you'll never make a cake or muffins without it again.

2 cups all-purpose flour

1½ teaspoons baking powder

1½ teaspoons baking soda

1 teaspoon mace

½ teaspoon cinnamon

½ teaspoon fine sea salt

4 eggs

1 cup sugar

1 cup vegetable oil

2 teaspoons vanilla extract

1½ cups pumpkin puree

⅓ cup maple syrup

½ cup dark chocolate chips,
    plus more for topping the muffins

For the crumble

1 cup all-purpose flour

1 cup sugar

½ teaspoon fine sea salt

1 teaspoon cinnamon

1 teaspoon mace

1 teaspoon vanilla extract

¼ cup canola oil

1. Preheat the oven to 350°F and grease or line the wells of a 12-cup muffin tin.

2. Stir together the flour, baking powder, baking soda, mace, cinnamon, and salt in a large bowl.

3. Using a stand or hand mixer, mix together the eggs, sugar, oil, vanilla, pumpkin, and maple syrup in a large bowl.

4. Stir the dry mix to the wet ingredients until just combined.

5. Fold in the chocolate chips.

6. Make the crumble: Whisk together the flour, sugar, salt, cinnamon, mace, and vanilla in a medium bowl. Add the canola oil, 1 teaspoon at a time, until the crumble holds together in small balls when squeezed, like wet sand.

7. Divide the batter evenly among the wells of the prepared muffin pan. Top the muffins with extra chocolate chips and crumble.

8. Bake for 25 to 30 minutes, until a toothpick inserted in the middle of one of the muffins comes out clean. Store in an airtight container at room temperature for 3 days or freeze for up to 3 months.

Chocolate Chocolate Chip Pumpkin Muffins

45 minutes | Makes 12 muffins

When my kids were little, it was hard to get them to try new fruits and vegetables. So I started baking delicious recipes using ingredients like zucchini, pumpkin, chickpeas—anything that could fit in my blender. In this recipe and the Pumpkin Doughnut Muffins (page 246), the pumpkin is there more for moisture, rather than for flavor. Pumpkin spice season means pumpkin is always associated with the same baking spices, but I use it to add texture and nutrients to baked goods, then play with the flavor. You can use any squash you want for this, but canned pumpkin is definitely easiest.

1½ cups pumpkin puree (a little less than one 15-ounce can)

4 eggs

1¼ cups sugar

1 cup extra virgin olive oil

2 teaspoons vanilla paste or extract

½ cup maple syrup

2 cups all-purpose flour

½ cup cocoa powder

1½ teaspoons baking powder

1½ teaspoons baking soda

½ teaspoon fine sea salt

1 cup dark chocolate chips

1. Preheat the oven to 350°F and grease or line the wells of a 12-cup muffin tin.

2. Add the pumpkin, eggs, sugar, olive oil, vanilla, and maple syrup to a blender. Pulse until smooth.

3. In a large bowl, whisk together the flour, cocoa powder, baking powder, baking soda, and salt.

4. Pour the batter from the blender into the bowl with the dry ingredients while stirring. Whisk together until smooth and no streaks remain.

5. Fold ½ cup chocolate chips into the batter.

6. Divide the batter evenly among the wells of the prepared muffin pan and top with the remaining ½ cup chocolate chips.

7. Bake for 30 minutes, until a toothpick inserted into the muffins comes out clean. Store in an airtight container at room temperature for 3 days or freeze for up to 3 months.

S'mores Bites

15 minutes | Makes about 24 bites

S'mores bites are more like an arts and crafts project than a recipe. It's a really fun way to get the whole family, even the littlest hands, involved. My kids love making these, although they probably love eating them more. Sometimes I'll ask if they want to help make them, and they'll say, "No, but can you make them?"

My favorite kind of pretzel for these are the square Snyder pretzels, but you can use the regular shape, too—just use three chocolate chips for stacking instead of four, so they can balance that top layer without anything toppling over. You have to be careful putting these in the oven, if you accidentally knock your arm on something chocolate chips will go flying and you'll have to redo everything. Whenever I make these, I keep them in a container on the kitchen counter until they're gone, which is never long.

1 cup Snyder's Snaps pretzels (or another flat, square pretzel)

⅓ cup dark chocolate chips (or any chocolate you have)

½ cup mini marshmallows

 Tip You can make these with any small candy you have (Rolos, Milky Way, and Snickers are great. It works better with candy that doesn't have a cookie inside of it). Like the Brown Butter Candy Cookies (page 239), these are great to make after Halloween.

1. Preheat the oven to 350°F, and line a baking sheet with parchment paper. Place a few rows of pretzels in a single layer across the parchment paper.

2. Place 4 chocolate chips on each pretzel, balanced in the holes, and nestle a marshmallow in the middle.

3. Carefully transfer to the oven and bake for 2 to 3 minutes, watching carefully, until the marshmallows are puffy and the chocolate chips are melted.

4. Carefully remove from the oven and push another pretzel on top to make a little sandwich.

5. Place in the refrigerator to cool. Store any leftovers in an airtight container at room temperature for 3 to 5 days.

Three-Ingredient Crunch(y) Bar

VEGAN

1 hour 15 minutes, including refrigeration | Makes 9 crunch bars

Sometimes, a handful of dark chocolate chips after dinner is all I need to satisfy my sweet tooth. Other times, I'm in the mood for the project that comes with making a delicious dessert. This is a treat that checks all the boxes: It's easy and gives you the perfect sweet-and-salty bite. A typical crunch bar is made with Rice Krispies, but I always have tortilla chips and love the added saltiness. If you're up for a little activity after dinner, make these.

One 12-ounce bag dark chocolate chips
4 cups tortilla chips
3 cups cornflakes
Flaky sea salt, to garnish

1. Line a 9 × 9-inch square pan with parchment paper.

2. Place the chocolate in a heat-safe bowl or in a double boiler. Set the bowl over a pot of simmering water over medium-low heat to melt, stirring occasionally. If you're using a metal bowl, be careful—it will get HOT. You can also microwave the chocolate chips in a microwave-safe bowl in 30-second intervals on medium heat, stirring frequently so the chocolate doesn't burn.

3. Gently crush the tortilla chips and cornflakes and add to a large mixing bowl. Don't crush all the way—you want a variety of sizes.

4. Pour the melted chocolate over the chips and cornflakes. Mix until they are thoroughly coated with chocolate.

5. Transfer the mixture into the prepared pan and sprinkle with flaky sea salt. Push into an even layer with parchment paper so your hands don't get messy.

6. Refrigerate for about 1 hour, until set, then cut into squares. Store in an airtight container at room temperature for 3 days.

Sugar Cookies

30 minutes, plus cooling time | Makes 36 cookies

These cookies are a defining recipe for me as a mom. I started making them at the Baked by Melissa office whenever I had time during the day. It made being in the office fun and added to the culture. When my kids were born, I thought about how I wanted them to remember their childhood and decided sugar cookies would play a role in that.

Making and decorating cookies makes me feel like a kid again, too. When the girls were really little (before they could help in a meaningful way), I'd make them for "my kids," but really, it was for me. I'd show them how I piped the icing on, doing it by myself. I enjoy it so much. Now that they're older and they're taking more accountability in the kitchen, I try my best to let my kids help. Sometimes it's hard to relinquish control and let them do it, even if (especially if) it's not how I would. I have to coach myself: *Just let them make a mess. It's okay to get sugar on the floor. Don't be nuts.*

I'm still at the beginning of my parenting journey, but these cookies are a good reminder of the game of tug-of-war that raising kids is. I've been making these cookies for years—way longer than my kids have even been alive. And now I have to watch my kids make their own decisions or mistakes, just like in life. These cookies have helped me become a better and more patient version of myself as a parent.

When they have friends over, I fill pastry bags with different colors of royal icing and cover the table with cookies and toppings for them to decorate. It's a great activity. They end up eating way too much sugar, but that's part of being a kid. It's a priority to let them have magical childhoods and make these, however they want.

10 tablespoons (1¼ sticks) unsalted
    butter, softened

¾ cup sugar

1 large egg, at room temperature

2 teaspoons vanilla extract or paste

2¼ cups all-purpose flour

½ teaspoon baking powder

¼ teaspoon fine sea salt

Tip Freeze portioned dough balls on a baking sheet, then transfer to a freezer-safe bag. When you want a cookie, bring the dough balls to room temperature and bake at 350°F for 7 to 9 minutes.

continued

1. Using a stand mixer fitted with the paddle attachment, beat the butter and sugar on high until light and fluffy, 2 minutes. Add the egg and vanilla extract and beat for 1 minute.

2. Add the flour, baking powder, and salt and mix on low until just combined.

3. Split the dough in half and shape into a square. Wrap tightly with plastic wrap and refrigerate for 30 minutes.

4. Line a baking sheet with parchment paper and preheat the oven to 350°F.

5. Remove the dough from the fridge and roll into a ¼-inch layer. Use cookie cutters to cut out shapes in the dough, rerolling as needed to use all the dough. Arrange the cookies at least 1 inch apart on the prepared baking sheet.

6. Bake for 7 to 9 minutes, checking on them every 2 minutes. You don't want the edges to get brown and too crispy. Remove from the oven and let cool before you decorate. Store cookies in an airtight container at room temperature for 3 days.

For royal icing

2 cups confectioners' sugar

4 tablespoons whole milk, at room temperature

½ teaspoon vanilla extract

Food coloring (optional)

Rainbow sprinkles

7. Make the icing: Add the sugar, milk, and vanilla to a large bowl and stir until smooth.

8. If desired, split the icing into small bowls and stir in food coloring.

9. Use the icing to decorate by spreading with a knife or offset spatula, or dip the cookies into the icing. Don't forget to add sprinkles!

What to Do with Your Dough

This is the perfect sugar cookie base recipe. It's easy to double or triple, and you can make it ahead of time and store it in the fridge for a day. The recipe also includes my royal icing recipe; here are my other favorite ways to use it:

- Make it into a **gingerbread house** (there are a lot of templates online)
- Form the dough into a log and **roll in rainbow sprinkles**
- Dye the dough different colors and piece together to make **tie-dye cookies** or **pinwheels.** Have fun with it!

Snickerdoodle Chickpea Cake

GLUTEN-FREE, DAIRY-FREE

1 hour | Makes one 8 x 8-inch cake

Like my Granola Bars (page 245), I make this cake all the time without even thinking about the recipe. I know it's easy for me to say, but I think you can get there, too. I shared a version of this cake in *Come Hungry*, and like so many of my recipes, it continues to evolve. This version is my new favorite. Like the original, it's packed with nutrients (there's a whole can of chickpeas in it!), which keep the cake moist and make you feel good about eating it. This one has the most delicious maple cinnamon swirl. There's no better flavor combination on earth. It's gluten-free, it's dairy-free, and I can literally finish this cake all by myself. (Let's keep that part between us.)

For the cake

2 large eggs
3 tablespoons coconut oil
2 teaspoons vanilla paste
¾ cup full-fat coconut milk
¼ cup maple syrup
3 medjool dates, pitted
1 can chickpeas, drained and rinsed
½ teaspoon fine sea salt
1 teaspoon baking powder
1 teaspoon baking soda
½ cup oats
½ cup almond flour
1 teaspoon ground cinnamon

For the topping

3 tablespoons maple syrup
1 teaspoon ground cinnamon
1 teaspoon vanilla paste or extract
½ teaspoon fine sea salt

1. Preheat the oven to 350°F, and line an 8 × 8-inch square pan with parchment paper.

2. Make the cake: Add the eggs, coconut oil, vanilla, coconut milk, maple syrup, dates, chickpeas, salt, baking powder, baking soda, oats, almond flour, and cinnamon to a blender and pulse until smooth.

3. Pour the batter into the prepared pan.

4. Make the topping: Whisk together the maple syrup, cinnamon, vanilla, and salt in a small bowl.

5. Drizzle the topping over the batter and use a knife to lightly swirl it around.

6. Bake for 35 to 40 minutes, until the cake is golden and springs back lightly when you push on it.

7. Let cool before slicing. Store in an airtight container at room temperature for 3 to 5 days or freeze for up to 2 months.

Chocolate Chip Blondies

1 hour 30 minutes, plus time to cool | Makes 9 blondies

My Aunt Janie always brought blondies over when my parents hosted. I think of her every time I make them. The pan you use can make or break this recipe (which I know from experience). A straight-edge metal square pan will give you the best, most gooey results. And you can't use the toothpick trick to test if they're done—if a toothpick comes out clean, they're overbaked. Keep them in the oven until they're golden on top but still feel slightly undercooked in the middle. And be sure to let them cool before you cut into them, otherwise it can get messy! When you get it right, though, there's nothing better—it's all the best parts of a chocolate chip cookie in one delicious bite.

12 tablespoons (1½ sticks) unsalted butter, softened

1 cup packed light brown sugar

½ cup granulated sugar

1 egg plus 1 egg yolk

2 teaspoons vanilla paste

1½ cups all-purpose flour

1 teaspoon baking powder

½ teaspoon fine sea salt

¾ cup dark chocolate chips, plus more for the top

Flaky sea salt, for topping

1. Preheat the oven to 350°F and line a 8 × 8-inch metal square pan with parchment paper.

2. In a stand mixer fitted with the paddle attachment (or using a hand mixer), beat the butter on medium speed until creamy, about 1 minute. Scrape down the sides of the bowl and add the sugars. Beat on medium-high until light and fluffy, 3 to 5 minutes.

3. Scrape down the sides again and add the egg, egg yolk, and vanilla. Mix again to evenly combine.

4. With the mixer on low, add the flour, baking powder, and salt, just until combined.

5. Stir in the chocolate chips.

6. Spread the dough into an even layer in the prepared pan and press extra chocolate chips on top.

7. Bake for 40 to 50 minutes, until golden brown. The blondies won't look fully cooked in the middle, but you want them like that so they stay gooey. Be careful not to overbake!

8. Cool the blondies completely at room temperature (I leave mine out, uncovered, overnight). Once cooled, sprinkle with flaky sea salt and slice into squares or rectangles to serve. Store any leftovers in an airtight container at room temperature for up to 3 days. You can freeze blondies, but I don't recommend it.

Banana Sponge Cake

VEGETARIAN

1 hour 30 minutes, plus time to cool | Makes one 10-inch cake

I grew up eating my mom's fluffy chocolate chip sponge cake. My kids love it now, too, and ask to eat it for breakfast. I let them, because as my mom would say, it's good for you (eight eggs!). You make it in a tube pan, which has little feet to keep the cake ventilated when you flip it. And no greasing required! Thank you, Mom, for inspiring this most delicious recipe. I love you so much.

8 large eggs
3 overripe bananas
½ cup avocado oil
½ teaspoon fine sea salt
2 teaspoons vanilla
1 teaspoon baking soda
1 teaspoon baking powder
1 teaspoon cinnamon
1¾ cups sugar
2 cups all-purpose flour

1. Preheat the oven to 325°F.

2. Carefully separate the eggs, placing the egg yolks in one bowl and the whites in another.

3. Combine the yolks and banana and beat with a hand mixer on medium speed until smooth.

4. Add the oil, salt, vanilla, baking soda, baking powder, cinnamon, and sugar, and mix again until smooth.

5. Slowly add the flour and mix again until no streaks remain.

6. Wash and fully dry the beaters. Beat the egg whites on high until they form stiff peaks (the peak should be able to stand straight when you lift the beater out of the bowl).

7. Fold the batter into the egg whites carefully, so you don't deflate them too much (this is what will help it rise).

8. Pour the batter into an ungreased 10-inch tube pan and bake for 60 to 65 minutes, until the cake springs back when you press it lightly.

9. Once you remove it from the oven, invert the cake in the pan over a tea towel on the counter. Let cool completely.

10. Flip the cake over and run a knife or offset spatula around the edges so the sides release. Remove the cake from the pan and slice to serve. Store leftovers in an airtight container at room temperature for up to 3 days.

S'mores Icebox Cake

30 minutes, plus cooling time | Serves 10 to 15

An icebox cake is a baker's secret weapon: minimal effort yet super impressive. And it doesn't require an oven, which is a huge advantage in hot summer months. I love desserts inspired by s'mores. The dessert itself can be messy, but the flavor combination is a classic. I've never met anyone who doesn't like it. That's why it was one of our first flavors at Baked by Melissa. I still bring it back every year. Make this the day before your next party to leave time for all the graham crackers to soften, and get ready to accept compliments.

1 pint heavy cream
¼ teaspoon fine sea salt
½ teaspoon vanilla
1 cup marshmallow fluff
1 cup hot fudge
1 package chocolate pudding, made according to package instructions and chilled
1 sleeve graham crackers

 Note

The size pan you use with icebox cakes is very flexible—you don't need to go out and buy a new one for this recipe. Use whatever square or rectangular pan you have. I find sharp, straight edges are easier with this recipe because you don't need to reshape the graham crackers to make them fit.

1. In a stand mixer fitted with the whisk attachment (or with a hand mixer), whip the heavy cream on medium until soft peaks form, 3 to 5 minutes. Add the salt, vanilla, and marshmallow fluff, and whip, until stiff peaks form, a few more minutes. Be careful not to overbeat.

2. Set up your station. Line a loaf pan with parchment paper and set up one bowl with the marshmallow whipped cream, another with the hot fudge, and a third with the chocolate pudding.

3. Line the bottom of the pan with 2 to 3 graham crackers and spread marshmallow whipped cream over it with an offset spatula or spoon. Cover that layer with more graham crackers, then top with hot fudge. Add another layer of graham crackers and top that with chocolate pudding. Repeat the graham crackers–whipped cream–graham crackers–hot fudge–graham crackers–chocolate pudding pattern until you run out of space in the pan or run out of fillings.

4. Cover the pan with plastic wrap and refrigerate for at least 24 hours, so the graham crackers soften. For the last 30 minutes, place it in the freezer so it's easier to slice.

5. When you're ready to serve, lift the cake out of the pan using the parchment and slice. Store leftovers in the fridge for up to 3 days.

Maple Tahini Caramel

VEGAN, GLUTEN-FREE

5 minutes | Makes 1/2 cup

Tahini is a staple in our kitchen. I use it in everything, from smoothies and baked goods to salad dressings and dips. I love that it's vegan and pairs well with so many other flavors, both sweet and savory. Maple, cinnamon, and tahini is one of my favorite combinations. If you have vanilla paste, please use it, and don't forget the salt. You really are in for a treat.

¼ cup tahini
1 teaspoon vanilla paste
½ teaspoon cinnamon
½ teaspoon fine sea salt
¼ cup maple syrup

1. Whisk together the tahini, vanilla, cinnamon, salt, and maple syrup in a large bowl until smooth.

2. Store in an airtight container in the fridge for up to 1 week, and use it to top ice cream, apples, or other treats.

Hot Fudge

GLUTEN-FREE

15 minutes | Makes 2 cups

Once you make this hot fudge, you'll never go back to buying it at the store. These simple ingredients come together to make a rich, decadent ice cream topping that will bring you back to your childhood. Yum.

1 cup dark chocolate chips
One 14-ounce can sweetened
    condensed milk
2 tablespoons butter
2 teaspoons vanilla paste
½ teaspoon fine sea salt

1. Place the chocolate, condensed milk, butter, vanilla, and salt in a small saucepan and melt over medium heat.

2. Use immediately or let cool slightly, then transfer to an airtight container. Store in the fridge for up to 1 week. Warm in the microwave before using to top ice cream or other desserts.

universal conversion chart

oven temperature equivalents

250°F = 120°C

275°F = 135°C

300°F = 150°C

325°F = 160°C

350°F = 180°C

375°F = 190°C

400°F = 200°C

425°F = 220°C

450°F = 230°C

475°F = 240°C

500°F = 260°C

measurement equivalents

Measurements should always be level unless directed otherwise.

⅛ teaspoon = 0.5 mL

¼ teaspoon = 1 mL

½ teaspoon = 2 mL

1 teaspoon = 5 mL

1 tablespoon = 3 teaspoons = ½ fluid ounce = 15 mL

2 tablespoons = ⅛ cup = 1 fluid ounce = 30 mL

4 tablespoons = ¼ cup = 2 fluid ounces = 60 mL

5⅓ tablespoons = ⅓ cup = 3 fluid ounces = 80 mL

8 tablespoons = ½ cup = 4 fluid ounces = 120 mL

10⅔ tablespoons = ⅔ cup = 5 fluid ounces = 160 mL

12 tablespoons = ¾ cup = 6 fluid ounces = 180 mL

16 tablespoons = 1 cup = 8 fluid ounces = 240 mL

acknowledgments

This book wouldn't be possible without my incredible global community on social media. Thank you all for inspiring new recipes, asking questions, and trusting me with your weekly meals. You make the world a more delicious place.

The inspiration for so many of these recipes started in my parents' kitchen, as they gave me the confidence to go after my dreams and told me I could do anything I set my mind to. Mom and Dad, thank you for always encouraging me to pull up a chair to help you fix dinner and for sharing your love of food with me.

To everyone on my team at Baked by Melissa, who works every day to bridge the gap between bite-size cupcakes and microchopped salads. I'm in awe of your drive, creativity, and dedication. Sam Hahn and Megan Reed, thank you for holding our hands every step of the way. This book wouldn't be possible without you.

It was a joy working with my editorial team again at Harper Influence: Lisa Sharkey, Maddie Pillari, and Lexie von Zedlitz. Thank you for believing in me since the beginning and empowering my creativity. And to Bonni Leon-Berman, who did such an incredible job bringing my vision to life with design.

To Anne Elder: your talent as a writer shines through every page, but your teamwork, willingness to do whatever it takes, and positivity truly set you apart. You are the definition of a team player; you lift up everyone around you, and I am so lucky to work alongside you every day at Baked by Melissa. Beyond all that, I'm proud to call you a friend. My entire family shares in that sentiment, especially my two daughters, who absolutely adore you. Thank you for pouring your heart into this book and for being a meaningful part of our lives.

To our incredible photographer, Ashley Sears—three books together and somehow you keep getting better. You just *get* it. I know I didn't make it easy this time around, but you absolutely nailed it. Every shot is stunning and even better than I envisioned. I feel so lucky to have worked with you for the past nine years. You bring so much talent, heart, and calm to every shoot, and I'm beyond grateful we get to keep creating magic together.

In addition to stunning photography, Ashley is incredibly gifted at pulling together an all-star team: the impeccable taste of our prop stylist Elvis Maynard; food stylist Scotty Fletcher, who put his heart into every dish; and Mace Vannoni, who brings great energy to every set she's on. It was such a joy working with all of you, as well as Lucy Krebsbach, Kayla Wong, Todd Henry, and Andrea Nguyen. Thank you all for sharing your talents with us to make every day so fun.

Thank you to Staub, Earlywood, OXO, perfectwhitetee, and Victorinox/Epicurean for providing some of my favorite kitchen tools for our photo shoot, and to Poppy Bee Surfaces and Surface Workshop for the incredible backgrounds and surfaces.

Figuring out what to eat for dinner every night is the hardest thing about being a mom, but Scottie and Lennie—you inspire me every day. Thank you for being my most frequent (and most honest) recipe testers. Watching you learn how to cook, chop, and nourish yourselves makes me incredibly proud. I'm so excited to have you all on this journey with me. And finally, to Adi, who has been by my side in the kitchen and in life for the most magical years. You know I married you for more than your mom's salad recipe.

OKLOVEYOUBYE!

index

about the author

Melissa Ben-Ishay is the cofounder and CEO of Baked by Melissa, the dessert brand celebrated for its bite-size cupcakes. Founded in New York City in 2008, Baked by Melissa has many stores around the city and ships nationwide, with Melissa personally developing over eighty flavors a year. In 2020, Melissa's recipes went viral on TikTok, inspiring millions of people to finely chop salads for the perfect ratio of flavors in every bite. Her second cookbook, *Come Hungry*, launched as an instant *New York Times* bestseller in 2024. She spends her time between NYC and Hoboken, trying to decide what to make for dinner.

HarperCollins books may be purchased for educational, business, or sales promotional use. For information, please email the Special Markets Department at SPsales@harpercollins.com.

hc.com

FIRST EDITION

Designed by Bonni Leon-Berman

Library of Congress Cataloging-in-Publication Data has been applied for.

ISBN 978-0-06-345163-6

Printed in Canada

26 27 28 29 30 TC 5 4 3 2 1